Cricket attracts f
example when a he
is one player well-e
hogs. Dealing wit
greater ingenuity a
age. This book also
play' and an inter
are other diverting stories: a match where all the players
were on horseback; a bowling analysis of 0–0–4–0;
286 runs off one hit and even matches which started at
4 a.m. or earlier. This collection will pass the time
during the breaks for rain and delight all followers of
cricket during the long winter months.

To my Chris,

      With love on your
birthday,

           Jayne /xx

1·9·84

This Curious Game of Cricket

This Curious
Game of Cricket

George Mell

Illustrated by BILL TIDY

London
UNWIN PAPERBACKS
Boston   Sydney

First published in Great Britain by George Allen & Unwin 1982
First published by Unwin Paperbacks 1983

UNWIN® PAPERBACKS
40 Museum Street, London WC1A 1LU, UK

Unwin Paperbacks
Park Lane, Hemel Hempstead, Herts HP2 4TE, UK

George Allen & Unwin Australia Pty Ltd
8 Napier Street, North Sydney, NSW 2060, Australia

Text © George Mell, 1982, 1983
Illustrations © Bill Tidy, 1982, 1983

British Library Cataloguing in Publication Data

Mell, George
    This curious game of cricket.
1. Cricket—Anecdotes, facetiae, satire, etc.
I. Title   II. Tidy, Bill
796.35'8   GV919
ISBN 0-04-796073-6

Set in 10 on 11 point Garamond by Red Lion Setters, London
and printed in Great Britain
by Cox and Wyman Ltd, Reading

Contents

Foreword by Brian Johnston

I don't know who it was who originally coined the well-known cricket cliché, 'Cricket is a funny game', but whoever it was would be delighted to have his opinion confirmed by reading this fascinating book. It is a splendid collection of funny (ha-ha) and funny (peculiar) things that have happened at cricket. George Mell covers a wide range of subjects – ambidextrous players, batsmen getting out on purpose, freakish dismissals, the weather (of course!), cricket's connection with music, royalty and women, and my own special favourite, animals.

Although we don't have cricketing adventures with such exciting animals as lions and snakes here in England, I do remember that once in a Test at Edgbaston a mouse ran onto the pitch and held up play. And during a memorable Headingley Test, Blowers (Henry Blofeld) announced that he could see a butterfly *walking* across the pitch!

George Mell has unearthed an amazing number of curiosities, including the match at Bromley in 1735 where all the players were on horseback. We know of course that in a Lord's Taverners' Match at Cranwell, Prince Charles once rode out to bat on a horse. But he at least abandoned the horse at the crease.

I myself once experienced a curious happening at which George Mell has not included. During the Headingley Test of 1953 a man walked past our TV commentary position carrying a ladder over his shoulder and with a lavatory seat round his neck like a collar. He disappeared under the football stand and reappeared ten minutes later, still carrying the ladder but minus the lavatory seat. We never solved the mystery. Where was this high loo which needed a ladder in order to fix the seat?

That will be one for George Mell's next book, but meanwhile I hope I have whetted your appetite for *this* one. I am sure that, like myself, you will enjoy the unusual happenings and extraordinary records. I am going to make certain that I always have a copy with me in the Test Match Special commentary box next summer. It will be a wonderful 'filler' when rain stops play. And what's more, I shall be able to stump Freddie Trueman with questions gathered from this book. So please, Mr Publisher, don't send him a complimentary copy!

Ambidextrous Players

Play at Taunton in July 1954 was relieved by a maiden century by Leslie Angell, the Somerset opening batsman, and by a strange bowling performance from Hanif Mohammad of Pakistan. He displayed unusual versatility by bowling four right-handed deliveries and two left in one over before lunch, a feat he repeated after tea.

...

Although players who bowl left-handed and bat right (or vice versa) are fairly common, cricketers who can switch from one hand to the other are quite rare. In 'The Charm of Cricket Past and Present' the author tells how C. E. M. Wilson bowled both right- and left-handed during Surrey's innings against Cambridge University in May 1895.

☆

Roy Webber's *Cricket Records* mentioned J. Harry, who played for Victoria v. South Australia at Adelaide in 1891–2 and varied his bowling in the same way.

...

Quite different was the Rev. John Charles Crawford who died in 1935 at the age of 85. In his obituary *Wisden* states that he could bowl very fast right-handed and slow with his left. More unusual, he could hit hard against weak bowling but sometimes relented against poor opposition and would bat left-handed.

☆

A more recent instance of ambidexterity occurred at Kettering during the Northamptonshire v. Gloucestershire match in 1962 when H. Jarman for the visitors bowled three balls with his right hand and then three with his left.

...

Bill Voce, the Nottinghamshire fast bowler, made the ball swing so disconcertingly in the match against Somerset at Taunton in 1930 that G. Hunt switched over to left-handed batting when facing him but batted in his normal right-handed manner against the other bowlers.

1

Animal Crackers

While members of Pertenhall CC, Bedfordshire, were having a practice game in May 1955 play ended unexpectedly. A cow picked up the ball in its mouth and swallowed it, apparently with no ill effect.

...

Frank Lane, noted writer on natural history subjects, wrote of a match at Nairobi in the days when the bush encroached very near to the town and a batsman drove a ball towards the boundary. As it was going over the line a lion jumped out of the bush and began playing with the ball. The fielders claimed 'Lost ball' but the umpires insisted that, as the ball could be seen, it wasn't lost. The batsmen crossed for an unrecorded number of runs before enough men arrived to chase off the lion and retrieve the somewhat chewed-up ball.

☆

Bees have often interrupted cricket matches. A low-level flight once compelled cricketers at Papatoetoe, New Zealand, to lie flat on the pitch until the swarm had passed (25 November 1947); bees routed two cricket teams and 300 spectators in a senior Transvaal match on 23 November 1957; and in June 1962 the Oxford University v. Worcestershire match at Oxford was interrupted by them. Some Worcestershire fielders took refuge in the dressing room and a bee-keeper was eventually summoned to remove the swarm.

...

The *Daily Telegraph* on 12 October 1967 told how a schoolboy during cricket practice at Cowell, South Australia, saw a poisonous snake slithering towards him. He ignored a ball that had just been bowled, stepped out of his crease and killed the snake with one swipe of his bat. Then he looked round to see if he had been stumped—but the wicket-keeper had vanished!

The *Children's Newspaper* for 21 April 1928 related how a cricket team at Montagu, South Africa, had to suspend play when one of a number of ostriches near the pitch darted forward and swallowed the ball. As it was the only ball available the game developed into an ostrich hunt. The bird was captured and its neck massaged and pummelled until it spat out the ball.

☆

In 1892 the MCC v. Yorkshire match at Scarborough was interrupted when a runaway horse and cart careered across the pitch.

...

A hedgehog on the field held up play in the match at Gloucester between Gloucestershire and Derbyshire in July 1957. When it would not be shooed away, wicket-keeper Dawkes carried it off the field in his gloved hands.

☆

A great flight of swallows stopped the Nottinghamshire v. Gloucestershire match at Trent Bridge in 1975 and devoured a plague of gnats that was troubling the players. And on one occasion when MCC played Rossall School a hare ran right across the pitch and J. T. Hearne deliberately bowled a ball at it, bowling one of the widest wides ever seen.

...

Almost every season a stray dog runs onto a county ground and interrupts play. But at Worcester in August 1889 when the home team played Derbyshire a pig rushed onto the pitch.

☆

Flies stopped play at Lord's in June 1957 and two Hampshire men, Jimmy Gray and Harry Horton, had to have attention when insects got in their eyes. Then the plague moved on to the Oval to annoy the 17,000 spectators there.

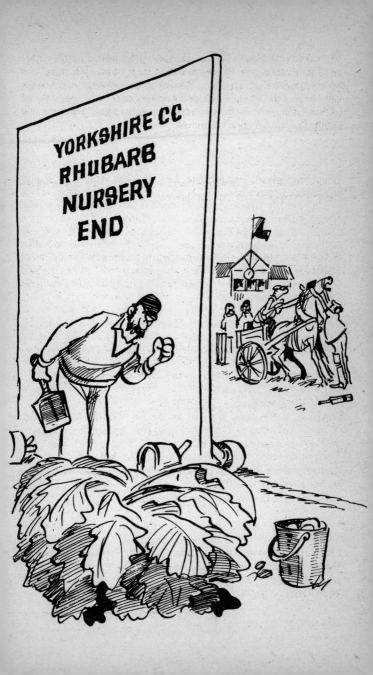

'Monkey Stops Play' was one newspaper headline on 22 December 1951 when MCC were playing Maharashtra at Poona. The animal ran onto the ground and sat down. Players tried to entice it into the slips but it evaded them. Then it made a dash for one of the umpires. Amid roars of laughter from players and spectators the official repelled it and the monkey at last departed and play was resumed.

...

When Kent played Hampshire at Canterbury in August 1957 play was held up when a mouse scurried onto the pitch. He raced after a four hit by Vic Cannings, the Hampshire bowler, and just missed being trodden on by Colin Cowdrey. Play stopped when umpire Charlie Elliott noticed him. The players could not entrap him and finally play was resumed when the mouse's schoolboy owner dashed onto the pich, dived on him and caught the errant mouse up in his school cap.

☆

In August 1978 a man watching a cricket match at Wrotham Heath, Kent, was taken to hospital after being bitten by a snake. Said the hospital doctor: 'It was a common British adder, and there is no need for any alarm.'

...

An unusual fate befell the ball hit by boys playing at Earlwood, Sydney, Australia, in October 1962. An elephant from a circus nearby was browsing at the edge of a cricket patch when a ball was driven towards it. The elephant fielded the ball with its trunk, swallowed it and the game ended.

☆

The now defunct weekly, *Answers*, once told how so many bees flew onto the ground in a Surrey v. Lancashire match at Old Trafford in June 1887 that players had to shelter in the pavilion until the swarm had vanished.

The Ball

When the cleaning of St Paul's Cathedral began in 1963 one observer reported that four cricket balls had been found by workmen, lodged in the carved scrolls on the west front. No one knew how they got there.

...

The poet Keats once got a black eye through being hit with a white cricket ball.

☆

In *The Cricketer* for 25 April 1959, it was said Warwickshire intended experimenting with a white ball in one of their early non-Championship matches, probably in a half-day game. Whether they did so, and with what results, wasn't reported, but apparently a privately organised party of English cricketers went to Paris in 1958 and played on the Parc des Princes using a white ball.

...

Fearful that ladies who took up cricket might be upset by blood-red cricket balls, one Kent manufacturer in 1898 produced some blue ones. Gamages advertised them but the balls were not popular as they blended too well with the sky. Apparently only one survived and was lent for display at Lord's.

☆

Cricket balls mounted with a silver shield recording outstanding bowling feats are quite common. The ball with which South Africa were dismissed for 30 runs at Birmingham in 1924 was cut in two and the halves, suitably inscribed, were presented to Arthur Gilligan (6.4 overs, 4 maidens, 7 runs, 6 wickets) and Maurice Tate (6 overs, 1 maiden, 12 runs, 4 wickets).

WHAT'S THE MESSAGE?

'WE KNOW THE GOVERNMENT IS IN SAFE HANDS'

On 1 December 1966 a relay of 200 cricketers threw a cricket ball two miles through Bridgetown as a tribute to the newly granted independence of Barbados. The ball contained a message of greeting from all the island's cricketers to Errol Barrow, the Prime Minister, and was thrown from the Test Cricket ground to the Government headquarters.

...

Playing against Worcestershire in 1955 Robin Marlar bowled three consecutive deliveries in one over with three different balls. The first two had been driven out of the ground and declared 'lost' as a result of big hits by R. G. Broadbent.

The spring annual of *The Cricketer* for 1963 described how the late G. W. Hammond, while on tour in Warwickshire, bowled and the batsman played the ball to mid-on who fielded it and threw it wildly so that the umpire had to take evasive action. Hammond stopped the ball and broke the wicket with the batsman well out of his ground but the umpire, unsighted, could not give a decision. When Hammond realised that the other batsman was out of his ground he hit the stumps at the other end but once more did not take a wicket as the square-leg umpire was watching events at the other end. To make matters worse, a ball was found nestling near the stumps at each end. One had fallen out of the umpire's pocket when he ducked but, as both balls were in approximately the same condition, it was impossible to decide which was actually being used in the match.

☆

During an MCC tour of Australia in the 1920s A. P. F. Chapman was presented with a gold cricket ball in a match against a local team at Bendigo, the once-famous gold-mining town.

...

In 1972, during the Haig National Club Championship, Pott Shrigley CC, of Cheshire, fielded first on a damp May day and experienced difficulty in holding the wet ball. The home side (unnamed in the *Guardian* report) had one slow bowler who had no trouble and when an umpire went to get some sawdust from a large pile at one bowler's end he discovered why. There were five perfectly dry balls at the bottom of the pile and the bowler was using them in turn.

Bats

Cricket bats, orthodox or otherwise, have always been made of wood with the exception of the metal one with which Dennis Lillee created a fuss during the first Test against England at Perth in the 1979–80 series. Almost simultaneously, and coincidentally, the Laws of Cricket were amended, decreeing that wood was the only material to be used.

...

Quite unusual is the bat that can be seen in Scunthorpe Museum. It is made of iron and is a product of the local ironworks. It weighs 9½ lbs, is two feet long and 2½ ins wide, the blade being only 11 ins long.

☆

In contrast, a Mr D. Cameron of Newry, Ireland, is said to have invented a pneumatic bat weighing only 1½ lbs.

...

During the final Test at the Oval against the West Indies in 1966 Tom Graveney scored 165 with a Panther Polyarmoured bat produced by Slazengers. This was an ordinary bat covered with a film of polymer plastic. In 1970 another novel bat was given some publicity. Carbon fibre instead of steel was used, which, it was claimed, 'could convert a two into a four and a four into a six'. Neither type of bat seems to have become popular.

☆

In an article in the *Sunday Times* in May 1967 Ian Peebles mentioned an unusual bat he had seen when he was a boy. This had a circular hole in the back of the bulge and, when the user had mastered the attack, he used to screw in a circular block of wood to gain extra driving power.

10

Jim Parks of Sussex used an unconventional bat in scoring 157 not out against Glamorgan at Hove on 12 May 1959. It had round shoulders instead of the usual square ones.

...

The present dimensions of the bat were established in 1774 when Tom White, playing for Reigate, Surrey, went to the wicket with a home-made bat so wide that it completely obscured his stumps. Opponents complained, with the result that the maximum width of 4¼ ins was established.

☆

Rather similar was the bat used in a single-wicket match at Bishop Auckland, Co. Durham, in 1876 by Mr M. Brown, a publican, who bet £20 to £100 that Mr W. Piers, an auctioneer, could not bowl him out in twelve hours, Brown to provide his own bat and Piers his own ball. *Lillywhite's Cricketers Annual* reported the match as follows: 'Great amusement was caused when Brown produced a bat specially made for the occasion, and was ten inches wide, exactly the width and height of the wicket.' Piers had obviously anticipated such a ploy for he arrived with a potshare ball weighing 27 oz similar to jacks used on bowling greens. Play began when Brown firmly placed his bat in front of, and completely obscuring, his wicket. The bowler attacked with his massive ball with such effect that 'in a short time the bat was beginning to show signs of being splintered. At length, by some accident, Brown left one wicket uncovered and the ball, coming straight, brought down the stump.' Piers had won in only 9½ minutes.

...

Bigger still is the concrete bat, 60 feet high, which was erected in Indore in 1971 to mark India's great victories over England and the West Indies. The players' names are inscribed on it in Hindi.

☆

When Yorkshire defeated the Rest of England at the Oval in September 1960 it was reported that Brian Stott for the county hooked a ball from fast bowler Sayer and found himself holding only half a bat.

George Brown of Hampshire, playing against Warwickshire at Southampton, had some disagreement with his captain, Lord Tennyson. As a result he went out to bat at the unusual position of no. 10 with something that was little more than a remnant of a bat. Almost at once he received a short, fast ball from Harry Howell and hit it over the wicket-keeper's head for six. Soon after the bat split as Brown made another powerful stroke. He then tore off part, gave it to the umpire and batted for the rest of the innings with half a blade.

...

When Majid Khan, of Glamorgan and Pakistan, was bowled for 28 by Ian Buxton of Derbyshire at Derby in August 1968, he strode into the pavilion and sawed the bat in two. 'I was getting a bit fed up with it,' he explained. 'I haven't made many runs with it lately.'

☆

In 1937 J. Knowles, of Nottinghamshire, created some sort of record by needing three bats to break his duck. He broke two and borrowed a third before he scored a run.

...

Some cricketers develop a real affection for their bats. James Broadbridge, of Sussex, carried his with him when he went for a walk; Ted Wainwright, of Yorkshire, took his bat to bed with him, while Daniel Day and John Bowyer, of Mitcham, Surrey, were buried with theirs.

☆

Among the archives of what was once the National Provincial Bank is a cricket bat cheque for the sum of £3−7−6 (£3.37½). Major Hedley of the 4th Queen's Own Hussars, hurrying to catch a plane to Germany, gave the bat to his father, asking him to have it rebladed. On discovering that he had no cheques he stuck a twopenny stamp on it (that was the charge on all cheques in those days) and signed it. As it fulfilled all legal requirements it was accepted by the bank without comment.

12

NO CHANCE OF LBW!

J. L. Carr in his interesting *Dictionary of Extra-ordinary English Cricketers* states that the game's oldest archaeological artefact is John Chitty's bat 'hewn in 1729'. He also tells of the Rev. Elisha Fawcett who went to the Admiralty Islands in the early nineteenth century to convert the inhabitants and, perhaps more successfully, to teach them how to play cricket. When he died his flock, too poor to pay for a monument over his grave, erected his wooden leg on it. It took root and grew so well that for many years cricket bats were cut from it.

...

Carr also refers to the Hon. Robert Grimston and his practice of going to the wicket with two bats – a large one for blocking deliveries from the mighty Alfred Mynn and a smaller one for thrashing bowlers of less skill.

In 1979 a cricketer tried to take his bat through the French customs at Calais. He explained what it was used for, but the official was completely baffled by it. He then handed him a list of a thousand items, inviting him to select a suitable category. Eventually the bat was admitted into France as an 'engine sportif sans mouvement mecanique' and a duty of 1.25 francs had to be paid.

☆

Customs officials examining a consignment of cricket equipment from Pakistan as it passed through New York in 1975 saw one of their specially trained dogs sniffing at one bat. They examined it and found that the blade had been hollowed and filled with £20,000-worth of hashish.

...

When women played the men of Potton, Bedfordshire, in September 1955 they used bats a foot wide. The game ended in a tie, both sides scoring 41 runs.

☆

In 1874 W. G. Grace once took a team to play F. Townsend's XI at Cheltenham, agreeing that he would use a broomstick while everyone else used bats of normal dimensions. Despite this handicap W.G. made the second highest score – 35.

...

Although Graham Roope, of Surrey, used a blue bat and Barry Richards, of Hampshire, a bright orange one in their John Player League matches one Sunday in June 1973, Roope was refused permission to use his pale blue bat in the second Test against New Zealand at Lord's.

☆

Nowadays quality bats can cost £50 and more, but in 1766, 'William Pett of Sevenoaks sold eleven bats at 2s 6d [12½p] ... to the Duke of Dorset.' (*Cricket* by Rowland Bowen.) By 1773 Pett's price had risen to 4s (20p) and by 1833 bats were costing 35p each.

In the early days of Australian cricket players up-country carved their own bats from solid cedar and cut balls from a fungus called 'black-fellow's bread'.

...

In *Six and Out* Ray Robinson wrote about S. G. Barnes: 'His clowning in a testimonial match for Sir Donald Bradman caused the biggest commotion. His chief trick was to throw aside his bat, produce a toy one from under his pullover and take block with it. The umpire was reluctant, but Barnes insisted that the toy bat was legal, as it came within the only dimensions laid down by the Laws of Cricket.'

☆

During E. G. Hayes' spell with Surrey he enlivened what the papers called 'a dull game' against Essex at Leyton by walking out to bat without a bat.

...

About 1910, says J. L. Carr in his *Dictionary of Extra-ordinary English Cricketers*, the poet, Edward Thomas, asked Mr Grundy, a Bearsted wheelwright, to make him a new wooden leg for the Welsh poet, W. H. Davies. He supplied a diagram so that it could be made in the desired shape but, as Grundy had not been told what the object was, he invoiced it as 'A Curiosity Cricket Bat'.

☆

The Gloucestershire v. XI of Cheltenham game on 15 August 1877 finished early, so the two teams played again to give spectators their money's worth. Gloucestershire batted with broomsticks and scored 290, E. M. Grace making 103, while the Cheltenham men used bats and had scored 50 for two wickets when the day's play ended.

Big Hits

Big hits can be measured in two ways: the distance the ball travels from hit to pitch; and the number of runs scored from it. The record for the former category is usually credited to Walter Fellows who, while practising on the Christ Church ground at Oxford, in 1856, drove a ball 175 yards, a feat not confirmed by measurements made at the time. C. I. Thornton, during practice at Hove on 25 August 1876, drove a ball near to where the cricket historian, the Rev. James Pycroft, was sitting. He marked the spot and measured the drive as covering 168 yards 2 feet.

...

G. J. Bonnor, the Australian big hitter, drove balls 160 and 149 yards at Melbourne and 147 yards on Mitcham Common, Surrey, in May 1880. This, too, was measured. A much more famous drive by Bonnor could not be measured. At the Oval in 1880, playing against England, he hit the ball to such a tremendous height that when Fred Grace caught it – in itself a very noteworthy feat – the batsmen had turned for the third run.

☆

Normally the most productive scoring stroke is the hit for six although occasionally overthrows give more runs to the lucky batsman. The record for such a hit is 11 runs scored by S. Wood, playing for Derbyshire, off the bowling of C. J. Burnup of MCC.

...

Next best is the nine-run stroke by Arthur Staples for Nottinghamshire against Northamptonshire, while Clem Hill, playing for Australia at the Oval against Surrey, once hit Tom Richardson for seven, eight and nine in two consecutive overs. The hapless fielder was Bobby Abel, who was so exhausted with his efforts that he did not gather the ball on the third occasion until the batsmen had almost completed the fifth run.

As might be expected, much bigger scores were made from single hits in the days when a ball was not considered lost if it could be seen. According to one history of the MCC, during a match in Australia a ball was hit high into the air and lodged in the junction of two branches in a tall tree. Everyone could see it and, while fielders were borrowing a shotgun and eventually shot the ball down, the batsmen trotted up and down the pitch 286 times.

☆

In a local match in Lancashire in 1898 a batsman hit a ball over a cliff. The umpire refused to signal 'Lost ball' and while the fielders climbed down and retrieved the ball the batsman scored 264 runs.

...

On 26 May 1894 Camberwell Albion, playing Peckham Pushers, scored 129 and left their opponents only 55 minutes for their innings. It was enough. The first ball was hit into a cleft in a tall tree and the openers ran up 93 runs before the ball was dislodged. Then as wickets fell the Pushers scored the runs needed for victory and won by four wickets.

☆

At Thorpe Perrow in Yorkshire's North Riding in 1885, 31 runs came from a single hit, a figure beaten at Ingleby Cross in the Cleveland Hills a few years later when the ball was driven down a steep slope and the batsman was credited with 34 runs while relays of fielders recovered the ball.

...

Slack 'fielding' brought 47 runs from a similar stroke at Chatham Lines, Kent, in the 1880s. One side scored 46 runs in its innings and their opponents won with a single hit. The ball rolled down a steep hill called the Brook and several fielders went after it, throwing the ball to each other in turn. Unfortunately some 'catches' were dropped, and each time the ball rolled back some distance while the batsmen continued to trot up and down.

Where a cricket ground is situated alongside a railway line the ball sometimes travels many miles — by train. Eddie Paynter once hit a ball out of the ground at Manchester into a truck on a passing train and it was carried to Liverpool. And C. B. Fry once hit a delivery from Ranji into a nearby marshalling yard and the ball disappeared forever down a funnel.

☆

Kendal Cricket Club ground is similarly situated and, many years ago, one big hit landed the ball in the engine cab of a passing train. In this case an obliging driver drew up beyond the station and returned the ball. On another occasion a ball hit from the same ground landed on a passenger train and was carried to Windermere.

. . .

A big hit of a different character was featured in an instructional film made by Sir Len Hutton in 1948 according to Johnny Wardle's book, *Happy-Go-Johnny*. Playing at Westcliff, Essex, Len was filmed making 76 not out, but the producer felt that he should have a completed innings. Filming resumed a few matches later at Bournemouth, when a Hampshire player threw a high ball in front of a sight-screen. One of his mates caught it and Sir Leonard was apparently out in Hampshire from a stroke made in Essex.

☆

At least one big hit, not necessarily remarkably big, has actually been framed. In 1912 the great Victor Trumper, playing club cricket in Sydney, hit a ball out of the ground and broke a window in a nearby shoe factory. As a tribute, the owners left the window as it was for over 50 years. In 1963 the South Sydney Rugby League Club bought the factory as an extension to their club rooms. Rather than destroy or repair Trumper's window they decided to mount it, frame and all, in his honour as part of their new building.

Some big hits are what might be called hypothetical. They haven't been made yet, although prizes have been offered to any batsman smiting a ball the specified distance. Many famous cricketers have played on the ground at East Molesey, which borders on the Thames. Games have been played there since 1693, yet no one has ever hit a ball over the river onto Tagg's Island. 'W.G.', Bobby Abel, Learie Constantine, Peter May, Ken Barrington, various members of Australian touring sides have all heaved mightily but without success. 'W.G.' nearly did it, dropping the ball onto a punt moored to the Island – just four feet away from the target. In 1953 prize money amounting to £1,200 was offered to anyone achieving the feat, half going to the striker and the rest to the East Molesey CC and the National Playing Fields Association.

. . .

In 1871 Norwood CC, in South London, announced that anyone hitting a ball out of their ground would win a barrel of beer. As recently as 1966 it had never been claimed, but the club always keeps a new barrel handy – just in case.

☆

And in 1971 officials at Sydney Cricket Ground announced that prizes totalling almost £2,000 would be given to the first batsman to shatter the new clock face on the pavilion. No one seems to have achieved the feat yet.

. . .

Gerald Howat in *Village Cricket* tells how on Beacon Hill, near Rottingdean, Sussex, 67 runs were scored off a single hit. The ball ran down to the nearby village and was retrieved by a relay system of fielders. At the last stage one of them threw the ball over the wicket-keeper's head so that it rolled down the other side of the hill.

Big Scores

As *Wisden* records, A. E. J. Collins in a school match in 1899 scored 628 not out in an innings spread over five afternoons out of a total of 833. Break-o'-Day made 911 at Hobart in 1901–2 when C. J. Eady over four afternoons knocked up 566.

...

A. E. Stoddart in 1886 scored the then highest individual total, 485, in an innings of 813 for 9 for Hampstead v. Stoics.

☆

Six and Out, compiled by Jack Pollard, gives the full score for the Melbourne University v. Essendon match in March 1898 when the University amassed the first 1000 total on record. The innings, which included one double century and four single hundreds, ran on to 1094, after which Essendon, presumably too tired to bat much, were all out for a miserable 76.

...

Not until 1922–23 was the 1000 mark exceeded again, when Victoria scored 1059 against Tasmania at Melbourne, of which W. H. Ponsford made 437, including 42 fours, in 10 hours and 20 minutes. The 1000 mark became something of a habit with Victoria, since at Melbourne in 1926–27 they scored 1107 against New South Wales who scored 221 in their first innings. Ponsford didn't do quite so well with a mere 352 but J. Ryder got 295 and H. L. Hendry and W. M. Woodfull each scored hundreds. In their second innings New South Wales were all out for 230 and lost the match by an innings and 656 runs, a margin 10 runs less than that by which they had demolished Tasmania four years previously. But New South Wales might well have thought that Victoria's mammoth score was only a flash in the pan. Only five weeks later the sides met again at Sydney. Woodfull, Ryder and Ponsford were among the five players not retained for that match and Victoria were dismissed for a paltry 35!

When the Ulster Club (Sydney) met Macquarie CC at Moore Park in 1874, they batted on four successive Saturdays to score 1238 runs for nine wickets. At that stage the Macquarie players, fatigued and fed up, asked Ulster to declare and let them bat. The Ulster skipper refused so their opponents walked off the field and the game was abandoned.

☆

While scoring 256 in an up-country game in Australia, Sir Donald Bradman hit 14 sixes and 29 fours and at one stage scored 100 out of 102 – in three eight-ball overs! The scorebook showed these figures:

first over: 6, 6, 4, 2, 4, 4, 6, 1
second over: 6, 4, 4, 6, 6, 4, 6, 4
third over: – , 6, 6, 1, – , 4, 4, 6.

...

When the Indian team, Holkar, declared at 912 for 8 wickets, six batsmen scored hundreds, against Mysore in 1945–46.

☆

In 1921 Northamptonshire had the following totals registered against them in successive matches: 616 for 5 dec. (Surrey at the Oval); 604 for 7 dec. (Essex at Northampton); 621 (Australians at Northampton); and 545 for 9 dec. (Essex at Leyton).

...

The biggest score ever made by any cricket team in England must surely be the 920 amassed by Orleans in August 1882 against the Essex side, Rickling Green (who were all out for 94). The second-wicket pair added 507, a Mr Vernon scoring 250 and Mr Trevor 338. The Rickling Green bowlers had toiled through 293 four-ball overs. The author remembers seeing the full score in an old *Lillywhite Cricketers' Annual*.

☆

One day in 1845 Great Bentley CC of Essex spent all day scoring 311 for 9 against Bures CC. Pleas for a turn at batting were ignored. In 1957 the two teams met again and this time Bures turned the tables, winning by two wickets.

In July 1881 W. N. Roe, playing for Emmanuel (Cambridge) against Caius must have counted his own score. At the end of his innings – 415 not out! – he told the scorers that he had actually scored 416 and that they must have missed one of his runs.

...

On 1 August 1885 Beckenham CC met Bexley CC on their own ground. Bexley, batting first, scored 77. Beckenham replied with 470 for no wicket, L. Wilson scoring 246 and W. G. Wyld 203, in only four hours.

23

When Colin Cowdrey scored 307 for MCC against South Australia at Adelaide in 1962–63 *The Cricketer* pointed out that it was not only the highest score of his career but the highest by any English player in Australia. That score had never before been made in first-class cricket and the only lower scores that had never been made (up to that time) were 289 and 298. The scores 320 and 323 also had not been achieved but since then A. L. Wadekar has scored 323 for Bombay v. Mysore at Bombay in 1966–67.

☆

And, according to a reader's letter in the *Wisden Cricket Monthly* for July 1981, batsmen in the England v. Australia Tests have between them made every score up to 124 and many from 126 upwards. So far no one has made 125.

Fast Scoring

One century in a day is usually enough for most batsmen, but some have done better than that. A reader's query in the *Daily Mirror* in August 1960 elicited the information that George Walton, playing for Northumberland against Cheshire in a Minor Counties Championship match, hit two hundreds on the same day – 21 July 1955. He scored 119 in the first innings and when his side was set 144 to win scored 102 not out in 51 minutes for Northumberland to win by eight wickets.

...

Better still was Ranji's hat-trick of centuries at Cambridge in his student days. *The Cricketer* reported on 8 July 1922 that he once made 128 for Cassandra on the second morning of a two-day match against Saffron Walden on Parker's Piece. Then for the Basinettes, another Cambridge club, he knocked up 132 on the same day and rounded off his day's work with 150 for another team against Christ's and Emmanuel on their pitch.

☆

Compton and Edrich's 424 unfinished partnership against Somerset at Lord's in 1948 occupied only 240 minutes, while Compton during the MCC tour of South Africa in 1948–49 took 300 off the N.E. Transvaal attack in 181 minutes, the last hundred coming in just 37 minutes.

'SALAD DOES THAT
TO SOME PEOPLE!'

The fastest hundred is still the 113 not out scored in 42 minutes by P. G. H. Fender for Surrey v. Northamptonshire at Northampton in 1930 (he reached his century after 35 minutes), but there have been some other amazing instances of hurricane scoring by batsmen who didn't reach the century mark. At Taunton nearly 60 years ago Frank Woolley received one ball before lunch, resumed at 2.15 and was out by 2.30 having knocked up 90. In three overs he hit Jack White and R. C. Robertson-Glasgow for 70.

...

Herbert Sutcliffe and Maurice Leyland took 102 runs off six overs against Essex at Scarborough in 1932. Four overs from Ken Farnes cost him 75 runs.

Not Out

In a Ranji Trophy match at Poona in 1948−49 B. B. Nimbalkar scored 443 not out for Maharashtra against Kathiawar. After lunch he went out onto the field with high hopes of beating the then highest individual score, 452 not out by Bradman. He was out of luck. His opponents said that they had had enough and the game fizzled out with Nimbalkar undefeated.

...

An article in *History Today* for June 1955 quoted an old report from the *Derby Mercury* about a Mr Osgothorpe of Sheffield 'of whom there is no record of his ever being dismissed'! In one match in 1772 he batted for several hours against the Sherwood Foresters 'and at last the spectators so hampered him that the match had to be abandoned'.

In 1953 the Australian bowler Bill Johnston during the tour of England was top of the batting averages although he was no. 11 in his team's batting order. He batted 17 times and was not out 16 times so that his run tally, 102, equalled his average for the season. His nearest rival was Frank Cameron, the New Zealand fast bowler, who was not out 20 times in his 24 innings on a tour of South Africa in 1961−62. He had a spell of 13 consecutive not outs but his season's total (49) and average (12.25) were way below Johnston's.

☆

When Simon Douglas-Pennant, Cambridge pace-bowler in the early 1960s, was clean bowled in the University's match with Free Foresters at Fenners on 14 June 1960, an alert reporter realised that this was his first dismissal in 13 consecutive innings and that his season's total and average at that time was 34.

Benefits

One subscription to one of W. G. Grace's several testimonials came from Max Beerbohm, the famous writer. He is said to have sent one shilling, 'not in support of cricket but as a protest against golf'.

...

Benefits for popular cricketers nowadays produce some tremendous amounts, but it wasn't always so. In 1934 Leicestershire arranged a benefit match for A. W. Shipman. 'Attendances were so poor,' reported *Wisden*, 'that the player found himself some £60 out of pocket as a result of the match. Happily this was cleared off by the proceeds of the ''Sportsmen's'' match. Other subscriptions came in later.'

☆

Another player to have a disastrous benefit was H. T. F. Buse of Somerset. His match against Lancashire in 1953 ended in one day, Lancashire winning by an innings and 24 runs.

...

In its obituary of Albert Edwin Trott in 1915, *Wisden* commented on yet another unfortunate benefit match, 'against Somerset at Lord's on Whit-Monday 1907 he came out with a last flash of greatness taking four wickets in four balls and finishing the game by doing the ''hat-trick'' a second time in the same innings. This was a feat without precedent in first-class cricket.'

The most surprising benefit match was that arranged for J. M. Read of Surrey, who had played 15 times against Australia. The Oval Test against Australia in 1893 was allotted to him but he didn't play in the match which brought him £1,200.

☆

Cricketers who are awarded benefits, profitable or not, should thank the old Kent batsman, James Seymour, for the fact that their gains are not subject to income tax. His benefit in 1920 brought him £939.85 and, following the due processes of the law, Seymour appealed to the House of Lords, where it was decided that the benefit was a 'personal gift' and not income arising from his employment. That judgement still stands.

...

George Geary, of Leicestershire and England, who died in March 1981 aged 87, had a second benefit in 1936. He chose his county's game against Warwickshire at Hinckley. His reward was a beggarly £10. Like Albert Trott, already mentioned, the beneficiary was largely responsible for his own misfortune by being too efficient, taking 7 for 7 in the first innings and 6 for 20 in the second.

☆

Although he was technically an amateur, W. G. Grace profited from a number of testimonials that were, in effect, benefits. He was paid £3,000 as captain of Lord Sheffield's team that visited Australia in 1891. A national testimonial in 1879 brought him £1,500 and in 1895, his great year, when he scored 1000 runs in May and hit his hundredth century, three funds were launched for him, bringing him £9,073. Today those sums would probably amount to £150,000.

31

Boundaries

Prior to 1910, when the Laws were changed to allow six runs for any stroke clearing the boundary without touching the ground, only strokes that sent the ball right out of the playing area counted six. Obviously many mighty hits by W. G. Grace and other stalwarts would have converted nineties into hundreds and their tally of runs and centuries would have been much higher.

···

One of the oddest boundary hits was made in the second Test at Lord's in 1921 when Jack Durston, the Middlesex fast bowler, ran up to bowl to Warren Bardsley with the score at 127. As his arm came over it brushed his thigh and the ball slipped from his hand and rolled to a standstill about halfway down the pitch. Durston ran to retrieve it, but Bardsley acted more swiftly and got to it first. He hit the stationary ball for four, one of the few instances of a 'dead' ball being hit to the boundary.

☆

Occasionally a fielder running full pelt to stop a ball crossing the boundary line just gets a leg to it and helps it cross the line. Something rather different once happened at Hove when Sussex were playing the West Indies. When N. I. Thomson hit a delivery from A. L. Valentine to square leg a black dog bounded on to the pitch, seized the ball and carried it over the boundary, hotly pursued by players and umpires. The four runs were credited to Thomson, not the dog.

···

An even stranger incident brought four cheap runs to a batsman on the Anslow ground, near Burton-on-Trent, in July 1963. The ball, hit into the air, seemed certain to drop into the hands of a waiting fielder when suddenly it zoomed over the boundary for four. It had hit one of the five electricity cables that straddle the ground.

While fielding for Victoria v. Queensland at Brisbane in 1976–77 J. K. Moss had his foot caught in a gutter while trying to cut off a shot from G. S. Chappell. While he was trying to extricate it the batsman ran four.

☆

Just before tea in one Warwickshire v. Oxford University match, Norman Horner played at a ball which went for four runs, which the umpire signalled as byes. During the meal the umpire had afterthoughts and credited Horner with four runs – perhaps the first time that a batsman has scored a boundary at the tea-table.

...

John Edrich, of Surrey, is the only batsman to have scored 200 runs in boundaries in a Test match. He did so at Leeds in 1965 against New Zealand. He hit five sixes and 52 fours in his 310 not out.

Bowlers

On 15 August 1966 *The Times* reported that equipment normally used for testing the speed of rifle bullets was used in the Midlands to test the speed fast bowlers can achieve. Wesley Hall, the West Indian, at 79.4 mph was a mere 0.4 mph slower than England's David Brown.

...

In 1978–79 cameras and computers were used to calculate the speeds of the world's fastest bowlers, eight having eight deliveries each. Jeff Thomson, tested at Perth, Western Australia, was the fastest, registering 91.86 mph with Michael Holding next with 87.76 mph. Imran Khan (Pakistan) was not far behind with 86.77 mph, closely followed by Garth le Roux (South Africa) at 86.58 mph. Dennis Lillee recorded 84.72 mph, but not one English bowler was in the first twelve. Apparently Bob Willis was unavailable, as was Rodney Hogg, but a previous check at Brisbane had shown that Willis at his best attained a speed of 74.30 mph, the same velocity credited to Chris Old. At the other end of the scale Bishen Bedi, tested at Lord's, delivers his specials at only 38.50 mph.

☆

When Jack Marsh, an aboriginal fast bowler, clean bowled Victor Trumper, in a State trial at Sydney Cricket Ground on 17 November 1900, one umpire decided that Marsh was a thrower and told friends that he would no-ball him next day. Marsh must have learned of this because, when the match restarted, he had been strapped up with a splint on his bowling arm. His doctor also gave him a certificate stating that he could not possibly throw while wearing the splint. The umpire watched him from square leg and had to agree that Marsh's delivery was perfectly fair.

Eddie Gilbert, the Australian aborigine, according to an unconfirmed story, was so fast that the wicket-keeper did not even see one of his deliveries. The long stop tried to stop it with his coat but the ball went right through and travelled another fifty yards, crashing through a wooden fence and killing a dog belonging to a spectator.

...

'Mad Charlie' was the nickname for Charles Brown, a Nottinghamshire player in the 1850s. 'Although he was a good batsman and a competent wicket-keeper his bowling was vastly different. He bowled from *behind his back*, the ball being propelled, at no inconsiderable pace, by a sort of whipping motion of the arm.' His deliveries were apparently very accurate and took some watching.

Fast bowler George Brown, of Brighton, who flourished about 1825, was so fast that his long stop, Little Donch, used to protect himself with a sack of straw tied to his chest.

☆

Alfred Shaw, who played for Nottinghamshire and Sussex in the 1870s, was such an accurate bowler that in all his career he did not send down one wide. Shaw, called the 'Emperor of Bowlers' by Richard Daft, bowled 25,000 overs in his long career. 7,000 of these were maidens. Playing for the North v. South at Nottingham in 1876 he bowled 23 consecutive four-ball maiden overs.

...

Taking all ten wickets in an innings is a rare enough feat but on the same day in 1921 J. C. White, of Somerset, and W. Bestwick of Derbyshire did that. Bestwick took 10 for 40 against Glamorganshire at Cardiff and White took 10 for 76 against Worcestershire at Worcester.

☆

Playing for some unspecified team against Nottingham City Transport, Roy Winfield, put on to bowl when the score was 39 for 3, took six wickets with his first six balls and caught the last man out from the first ball of the other bowler's next over. His analysis was 6 wickets for 0 runs and the opposing side slumped from 39 for 3 to 39 all out.

Hat-tricks

Almost always hat-tricks are performed by regular bowlers but A. C. Smith's three in three balls for Warwickshire v. Essex at Clacton on 6 August 1965 was different. He was a wicket-keeper who occasionally did a bowling stint. Other unusual hat-tricks included W. H. Brain's feat of stumping three Somerset batsmen off the bowling of C. L. Townsend for Gloucestershire at Cheltenham in 1893. H. Fisher, of Yorkshire, dismissed three Somerset men with successive deliveries, all lbw, in 1932 and J. A. Flavell did likewise for Worcestershire v. Lancashire at Manchester in 1963. When H. L. Jackson performed the feat for Derbyshire v. Worcestershire at Kidderminster in 1958 he was aided by his wicket-keeper, G. O. Dawkes, who caught all three. When S. G. Smith took three in three balls for Northamptonshire v. Warwickshire at Birmingham in 1914 all three batsmen were caught by G. J. Thompson.

...

'Same Again' was the newspaper headline in March 1963 when Ralph Lindsay, playing for Oudtschoorn against Port Elizabeth in a South African match, dismissed Voges, Jones and Le Grange in three consecutive deliveries. In 1957, on the same ground and against the same opponents, he achieved a hat-trick and his victims were the same three men in the same order.

☆

Several bowlers have performed delayed hat-tricks – two wickets in two balls and then another first ball either after the tea interval or on the next day. But in his book. *Fast Fury*, Freddie Trueman tells how Ken Taylor, playing for Yorkshire against Pakistan in 1954, ended their innings by having Shujauddin and Khalid Hassan lbw to successive deliveries. He was not asked to bowl again until Yorkshire played Surrey when, with his first ball, he had Tom Clark caught by Yardley at mid-wicket off a full toss. Freddie asks, 'Now was that a hat-trick?'

*At Sleaford on 20 August 1892, a Mr Aitken for the local side clean
bowled three men with successive balls, each time breaking a stump in
halves – the leg, middle and off stumps respectively.*

…

Inevitably in minor cricket double hat-tricks and at least one *treble* hat-
trick have been performed. Gerald Ziehl, a Rhodesian all-rounder,
took six wickets in one over on 19 March 1952 at Salisbury,
Rhodesia, finishing with 9 wickets for 4 runs in four overs. Playing for
Stainton, near Penrith, 16-year-old Brian Hill dismissed six Staffield
batsmen with six successive balls, four in one over and two in the next.
Even more impressive was the feat mentioned in the *Daily Mirror* on 5
December 1967. Stephen Fleming, 14 years old, took nine wickets
with nine successive balls playing for Marlborough College against
Bohally Intermediate at Blenheim, New Zealand.

☆

The History of Radley College tells of W. E. W. Collins, 'a huge hitter
and ferocious bowler', who claimed to have dismissed three men with
one delivery. 'The first victim was hit on the thumb and was led out
bleeding profusely, his colleague fainted and the next man in decided
not to bat.'

Strange Analyses

John Kelly of Derbyshire achieved a remarkable analysis against Lancashire at Old Trafford on 5 July 1955 and the press gave it some prominence. It read:

O.   M.   R.   W.

0   0   4   0

His first and only delivery was a no-ball, hit for four by Jack Dyson.

…

Playing in an unofficial Test against New Zealand in 1935–36, J. H. Human had figures of 1–1–0–0 yet conceded 24 runs. For tactical reasons his over included six deliberate wides to the boundary.

☆

A note from Roy Webber in the *Daily Telegraph* for 20 April 1957 told how during a Sheffield Shield match between Victoria and New South Wales a strange paradox resulted. C. G. Macartney took 2 for 43 in the first innings (average 21.5) and 4 for 6 in the second (average 1.5). M. A. Noble took 1 for 32 (average 32) in the first innings and 6 for 21 (average 3.50) in the second. Although Macartney had the better average in both innings his match average, 8.16, was inferior to Noble's – 7.57.

…

Some theoretical averages show odd results, at least to non-mathematicians. The *Telegraph*, following the item already quoted, also pointed out that, if two bowlers towards the end of a season have each taken 28 wickets for 60 runs and in the next and last match one takes 4 for 36 and the other 1 for 27, it would seem that the man with 4 for 36 must have the better average. Not so. They would end the season with 32 wickets for 96 and 29 wickets for 87 respectively, each averaging three runs a wicket.

In his book *Cricket Records* Webber relates A. E. Relf during the MCC's 1905–06 tour of South Africa had identical averages for both batting and bowling. He scored 404 runs in 16 completed innings and took 16 wickets for 404, averaging 25.25 for each.

☆

Playing for Warwickshire v. Northamptonshire at Northampton in 1938 Eric Hollies returned these two analyses:- 30–7–66–6 in the first innings and 30.3–9–66–6 in the second.

...

Playing for Middlesex v. Nottinghamshire at Nottingham in 1882 W. Clark returned the analysis of 25.2–24–3–1. A shot for 3 was the only scoring shot made off him in 102 deliveries.

☆

One of the most astonishing bowling analyses on record was returned by R. G. Nadkarni in the India v. England Test at Madras in 1964. It read 32–27–5–0 and, according to reports, English batsmen said that he was 'unhittable'.

Caps

In *Famous Cricket Grounds* Laurence Meynell tells how William Henry Scotton, the Nottinghamshire stonewaller, who once batted for an hour without scoring a single run, scored five very quick runs by a fluke. Playing against Middlesex at Trent Bridge in 1891 he hit the ball hard as the bowler's hat fell from his head. The ball hit it in mid-air and the umpire correctly awarded Scotton the five-run penalty.

...

More exotic was the turban worn by Swaranjit Singh, the Cambridge University all-rounder of the 1950s. He was fond of telling how the turban once got him a wicket. 'It dropped off as I was delivering a ball,' he said, 'and a mesmerised batsman was given out leg before.'

☆

Playing against the Prime Minister's XI in Australia in February 1959, Colin Cowdrey tried to get out as soon as he had scored a century and lofted a sitter to square leg where Lindsay Hassett dropped it. Hassett, reports continued, borrowed the umpire's panama hat and Cowdrey promptly skied another towards him which was caught in the hat.

...

A. V. Mankad, facing a bouncer from Chris Old in a Test match in July 1974 at Edgbaston, lost his cap as he tried to fend off a ball. It dropped onto his wicket, knocked off a bail and Mankad was out, hit wicket.

'Surrey's Pakistani batsman Younis Ahmed hit the most unusual six of his career', said the *Daily Express* on 26 August 1972, when he played a ball to cover for a single. The fielder, Lawrence Williams (Glamorgan), playfully threw his sun-hat at the ball, slowing it down. Younis was then given an extra five runs.

☆

A letter in *The Cricketer* for 2 July 1965 described an odd incident in the Harrow School v. Winchester match at Harrow a few days earlier. A bouncer from C. A. Holt hit the batsman on the head, dislodging his cap which fell on the stumps 'where it hung suspended as though from a peg in the dressing room'. Neither bail was removed and the batsman, R. L. Burchnall, went on to make 141 before being dismissed. The letter writer was umpiring at the bowler's end when the incident occurred.

Frank Hayes, Lancashire captain, thought he had reached 1000 runs for the season when, playing against Yorkshire on 26 August 1980, a delivery from Phil Carrick struck a safety helmet placed behind the wicket-keeper. He was credited with five runs, but after tea it was realised that Hayes had not struck the ball, so the five went down in the scorebook as extras. And Hayes was out without adding to his score.

...

Years ago, while Sussex were batting at Cheltenham, Tom Goddard stopped the ball with his cap when it was being returned to the bowler. 'The action was unpremeditated,' said a newspaper report. Goddard happened to have his hat in his hand at that moment and let the ball roll into it, giving a bonus of five runs to the lucky batsman.

Complaints

Richard Daft in his book, *Kings of Cricket*, published in 1893 when the telephone was in its infancy, wrote: 'The telephone is a splendid invention, speaking generally, but I cannot help wishing it had never been utilised on the cricket field. The falling off of gates is, I believe, in a measure owing to this. People within a few miles of the ground can be kept so well posted up in the progress of the game without going to witness it that many do not favour us with their presence at the matches themselves.'

...

A match arranged at Tilbury Fort, Gravesend, in 1776 between Kent and Essex cricketers never started when one of the visitors complained that Kent had included in their team a player who was ineligible. Feelings ran high and a fight broke out. When a Kent man saw that one of his friends was getting the worst of it he ran into the guardroom, seized a gun and killed one of the Essex men. This frightened the rest, who rushed to the guardroom and armed themselves. Soldiers on duty could not restrain the infuriated would-be cricketers who began firing on each other. A bystander was bayoneted and the sergeant in charge of the fort was shot dead. As the pitch began to look more like a battle-field the Essex men panicked and ran off over the drawbridge, while the Kentish men withdrew across the river.

☆

The *Penny Morning London Advertiser* for 6 July 1844 sounded off as follows: 'Cricket Imposition; 6d. Entrance Fee. Last Wednesday a great Cricket Match was played in the Artillery Ground by 22 picked gentlemen from most counties in England, but the small appearance of Company is plain proof of the Resentment of the Publick to any imposition; for the Price, on going into the Ground, being raised from Two Pence to Sixpence, it is thought there were not 200 Persons Present; when before they used to be 7 or 8,000; which plainly verifies the Old Proverb; All Covert [*sic*] All Lose.'

In somewhat similar vein Wilfred Wooller, then secretary of Glamorgan County Cricket Club, was reported in *The Times* of 13 June 1972 as taking 'an unusual step to register a protest at the way Somerset were conducting their innings at Swansea yesterday. He announced over the public address system that if any spectator felt he was not getting value for money an application for a refund would be sympathetically considered.'

...

PUBLICK CRICKET MATCHES

Cricket is certainly a very innocent and wholesome exercise yet it may be absurd if either great or little people make it their business. It is grossly abused when it is made the subject of public advertisement to draw together great crowds of people who ought, all of them, to be somewhere else. Noblemen, gentlemen and clergymen have certainly a right to divert themselves in what manner they think fit, nor do I dispute their privilege of making butchers, cobblers or tinkers their companions. But I very much doubt whether they have any right to invite thousands of people to be spectators of their agility at the expense of their duty and honesty. The diversion of cricket may be proper in holiday time and in the country; but upon days when men ought to busy, and in the neighbourhood of a great city, it is not only improper but mischievous to a high degree. It draws numbers of people away from their employment to the ruin of their families. It brings together crowds of apprentices and servants whose time is not their own. It propagates a spirit of idleness at a juncture when, with the utmost industry, our debts, taxes and decay of trade will scarce allow us to get bread. It is a most notorious breach of laws as it gives the most open encouragement to gaming.

The Gentlemen's Magazine, September 1743.

Cricket Clubs

Virtually unknown in the annals of cricket are the Untouchables CC, unheralded and unsung except for a paragraph in what was the *Manchester Guardian* on 27 June 1956. In what was then their twelfth season the club had played 127 games in north-east Lancashire, 109 had been lost and the remainder drawn. In the previous season, the captain stated at the annual dinner, the club had come nearer than ever before to a victory. 'With six wickets to fall and only nine runs to make, there really did seem a chance of pulling it off.' Alas, it was not to be.

...

The much more famous I Zingari (the Italian for 'The Wanderers') were founded in July 1845 and for a while fielded one of the most powerful sides in England. They once beat the Australians. The club follows three principles: keep your promise, keep your temper and keep your wicket up. One of the club's rules specifies that 'the entrance be nothing and the annual subscription shall not exceed the entrance'.

☆

In 1956 documents were found proving that Newport Pagnell CC in Buckinghamshire was founded in 1824 and among its playing members were the Marquess of Chandos and the Earl of Euston. Each member paid a match fee of one shilling but the winning side had their money refunded. One of the rules ordained that 'cold meat and ale shall be provided from two to three o'clock on every day of meeting, by some Innkeeper'.

Older still is the Sevenoaks Vine club, founded in 1734. Its ground, called the Vine, is in the middle of the town and in its first year Kent and Sussex played there. The second Duke of Dorset captained Kent, and Sussex were led by Sir William Gage. There was a sidestake of a guinea a man, quite a modest stake for those days. The ground was presented to the town by Lord Sackville, but later it was agreed that the Vine should pay an annual rent to the current Lord Sackville. It can sometimes be seen on a billiards table in Knole, the Sevenoaks stately home. It consists of one cricket ball.

...

According to Gerald Howat in *Village Cricket*, Cuckfield CC in Sussex was in its early days sponsored by Thomas Sergison, a local aspirant for a seat in Parliament. He put up 40 guineas for a match in the village, hoping to secure more votes in the 1741 election. Unfortunately the benefactor was beaten by a candidate supported by the powerful Duke of Newcastle. He continued to support the cricket club, however, and to this day it pays only a peppercorn rent to his descendants for the right to play in Cuckfield Park.

Debuts

On his Test debut at Sydney in 1903–04 R. E. Foster scored 287, which is still the highest score made by an Englishman in a Test in Australia.

...

Denis Compton made his debut for MCC in a match against Suffolk at Felixstowe. On his arrival at the ground he realised that he had left his cricket bag at Lord's and played in borrowed kit. He used the kit belonging to a player seven inches taller than himself who also took 2½ sizes larger in boots. In the first innings Denis was bowled first ball, but in the second, when his own kit had arrived, he scored 110.

☆

Fast bowler W. E. Bowes, of Yorkshire, made his debut for MCC against Cambridge University at Lord's and did the hat-trick.

...

One morning in the 1890s H. I. Young, a young sailor on leave, arrived at the Leyton cricket ground long before a county match was due to start and watched net practice. When the Essex captain, H. G. Owen, was waiting for a bowler, Young volunteered. He bowled so well that Owen, learning that he was born in Leyton, asked him to play there and then for the county. Young, later nicknamed 'Sailor', turned out in borrowed kit and did so well that Essex CCC bought him out of the navy. He played for the county for many years and was chosen for England v. Australia in the 1899 series.

☆

On his debut for Warwickshire J. M. A. Marshall, playing against Worcestershire at Dudley in 1946, began with a legitimate 11-ball over. He took a wicket with the last ball of an over and the umpire allowed him to bowl five more before realising his mistake and calling 'over'.

R. R. Phillips, making his debut for Border v. Eastern Province in South Africa in 1939–40, achieved the hat-trick in his first over. He had previously played four matches and never bowled.

...

Freddie Stocks, the Yorkshire-born all-rounder who played for Nottinghamshire, took a wicket with his first ball in first-class cricket against Lancashire at Manchester in 1946 after his first Championship innings, against Kent at Nottingham, had brought him a score of 114 – a unique double.

☆

J. M. Allan for Oxford University bowled seven consecutive maiden overs against Yorkshire at Oxford in 1953 and bowled three more against the Australians, taking the wickets of K. R. Miller and I. D. Craig before conceding his first run in first-class cricket in his eleventh over.

...

The most sensational debut in county cricket was that of Harold Gimblett in 1935. He was given a trial by Somerset but was not considered good enough and was sent home from Frome. The next day a last-minute vacancy arose in the team to play Essex. Gimblett was recalled, went in at no. 8 when Somerset were 107 for 6 and struck 123 out of 175 in 80 minutes. He reached the 100 mark in only 63 minutes and his maiden first-class innings was the fastest century of the season.

Catches

Batsmen cannot be caught out off fielders' protective helmets, but they can be caught off their own heads as many instances which have been reported in the daily press demonstrate. As far back as 1889 H. T. Arnall-Thompson, playing for Leicestershire v. MCC and Ground at Lord's, played a ball from Shacklock which flew off the edge of his bat, onto his eyebrow and rebounded to the bowler who thus achieved an unusual caught-and-bowled.

...

Ray Illingworth, playing at Lord's in his Yorkshire heyday in May 1960, was caught off his cheek. More often players are caught off a fielder's head. Charles Palmer, of Leicestershire, playing against Surrey at the Oval in May 1964, hit a ball from Lock onto the head of McIntyre, keeping wicket, and it rebounded to give an easy catch to a leg-side fielder. Oddly enough Palmer was out in exactly the same way against Surrey in the previous season.

☆

Some catches are made by fielders who know very little about it. During the second Test at Kanpur in 1959 Neil Harvey, Australia, caught Nari Contractor off a ball he never saw. He was fielding at short leg when the Indian pulled a delivery from Alan Davidson in his direction. Harvey turned his back and ducked, and the ball stuck between his thighs.

...

H. F. Nelson, batting for Northamptonshire against Sussex at Northampton in July 1938, cut a ball from J. Cornford onto the wicket-keeper's foot and it rebounded to first slip where H. E. Hammond took an easy catch.

In 1947 Alf Gover, playing for Surrey v. Hampshire, took an even more remarkable catch. At the end of his over he moved to short leg and was wriggling into his sweater when Jim Laker began bowling to Rodney Exton. Exton played an off-break to short leg where Gover was still enveloped in his sweater. The ball hit him between the legs just above the knees and he locked them together in a reflex action – and the ball stuck!

☆

During the Gloucestershire v. Kent match at Cheltenham in August 1965 Syd Russell snicked a ball from Alan Dixon and it lodged between his legs. Alan Knott, the Kent wicket-keeper, darted in front of him, caught the ball as it fell and claimed successfully for a catch. Just as quick was Haydn Davies, the Glamorganshire 'keeper, in 1952 when 'Dusty' Rhodes, the Derbyshire all-rounder, snicked a ball in the same way. As Rhodes opened his legs Davies caught it.

Few cricketers make catches to dismiss one of their mates but, as Ian Peebles relates in his biography of Patsy Hendren, the old Middlesex star once did that while playing in a country match in Australia. While watching a game he was asked to play and, agreeing to do so, was stationed in the deep at the bottom of a steep slope so that he could see nothing of the game. He was kept fairly busy and eventually caught a high drive. Not until later did he learn that he had caught out one of his own side.

...

According to the scorebook of the Gloucestershire v. Hampshire match at Southampton in 1919, Harry Smith, the wicket-keeper, made a catch contrary to the Laws of the game. Pothecary, Hampshire's last man, played a ball from Parker into the top of his pads when, in accordance with Law 33B, it was 'dead'. Smith caught it when the batsman shook it out, appealed and Pothecary was given out.

☆

Another batsman to lose his wicket through an umpire's error was the much more famous smiter, E. Alletson of Nottinghamshire, who at Brighton in May 1911 knocked up 189 out of 237 runs in only 90 minutes, including 34 runs in one over from E. H. Killick, who kindly included two no-balls in it. Less well known is the fact that Alletson might have scored many more runs. Maurice Golesworthy's *Encyclopedia of Cricket* says that when he was caught by C. L. A Smith off Cox 'many considered Smith was standing outside the boundary'.

...

At least one catch allowed by the umpire was made by a spectator! A Kent county magazine published some years ago tells how W. G. Grace was batting at the Adelaide Oval in 1874 when he hit a ball that sailed over the boundary chains. A young bank clerk, Alexander Crooks, leaned far over the boundary chains and caught the ball. W.G. expected the umpire to signal six but was enraged to be given out. As a result of this, the writer stated, Crooks became famous and later was appointed Treasurer of the South Australian Cricket Association.

During Victoria's mammoth innings of 1107 in 1926 on the Melbourne Cricket Ground, Arthur Mailey was hit for 362 runs in taking 4 wickets, with no maidens in 64 overs. Chaffed about his average, Mailey replied: 'If that chap in the brown derby at the back of the grandstand had held his catches I'd have had them out days ago.'

☆

In 1829 James Broadbridge literally threw his bat at a wide ball and was caught at point by Mr Ward.

...

An odd item was given prominence in some papers on 15 March 1959. At Wellington, New Zealand, R. C. Kearns, playing for Kilbirnie, cut a ball from K. W. Burke and the fielder at gully tried to intercept it but misjudged its flight. The ball hit him on the toe, ran up his trouser leg and stayed there. Carefully he removed it, appealed and Kearns was given out.

☆

A remarkable catch was reported from Dublin in 1844 when a Captain Adamson left his place on the boundary to speak to a lady in the crowd. Just in time he jumped back over the four-foot spiked fence and took a left-handed catch in mid-air.

...

Playing for the South v. North at Lord's in 1900, P. F. (later Sir Pelham) Warner drove a ball back to E. Smith who managed to turn it onto W. G. Grace's back, batting at the other end. From there it rebounded into Smith's hands for him to take a caught-and-bowled.

☆

Wisden reported the death of John Sharp on 27 January 1938, mentioning that he was upset by the attitude of the crowd when, playing for Lancashire at Old Trafford, he missed a catch off a stroke from H. W. Lee, Middlesex. He said he would never play there again and, although the Lancashire committee persuaded him to change his mind, at the end of the season he submitted his resignation.

54

In 1949 George Harpole, playing for a local club in Tampling, hit a ball onto the bent back of his partner's runner, where it remained to be taken by mid-off who was credited with a catch.

...

Wisden for 1908 gave details of E. M. Grace's feats on the cricket field. In 1906, playing for Thornbury, he took 352 wickets. In the following year, at the age of 65, he took only 212 'but had 208 catches missed off his bowling!'

☆

An unpublished book by G. B. Buckley, quoted by Rowland Bowen in his *Cricket*, tells of the 'most remarkable performance known to the history of the game'. A player at slip caught all ten batsmen at the same end and from the same bowler. Unfortunately names of the teams and the ground where the incident occurred were not given.

Freakish Dismissals

Barry Jarman, of Australia, was in the news on 4 August 1964 when the tourists met Glamorgan. The umpire at the bowler's end gave him out caught, and the other umpire gave him out stumped. He appears in the scorebook as caught by the wicket-keeper, E. W. Jones.

...

Years ago, when Surrey were playing Nottinghamshire, a ball from Neville Knox, a very fast bowler, whizzed past James Iremonger's stumps so close that a bail was removed. No one heard the ball touch the wicket. Fielders were emphatic that it had not touched the stumps and the umpire assumed that wind from the fast-travelling delivery had dislodged the bail so Iremonger was given out – bowled.

☆

In his book *Cricket Records*, Roy Webber recalled how M. P. Donnelly, the New Zealand left-hander, playing for Warwickshire at Lord's in 1948, was clean bowled by a ball that broke his wicket from the rear: 'A ball from J. Young hit Donnelly on the foot and bounced over his head, landing about a foot behind the stumps, only to break back towards the wicket. It can only be assumed that the ball landed in a bowler's footmark.'

...

Bernard W. Bentinck, playing for Alton CC (Hampshire), was bowled by a ball from H. E. Roberts, the Sussex professional, which hit a swallow on the wing and was deflected on to his wicket. The bird was killed.

During the Non-Smokers v. Smokers match played at Melbourne in 1887, Scotton for the Smokers had to receive the last ball and was anxious to obtain it as a memento of the match. He played it gently to point and ran to pick it up. The Non-Smokers appealed and Scotton was given out 'Handled the ball'.

☆

In his *Cricket Records*, Roy Webber mentions the case of A. Fairbairn, of Middlesex, in a match against Derbyshire at Derby in 1947. He was given out both caught and stumped by G. Dawkes, both umpires giving him out.

...

The same authority tells how F. H. Vigar, batting for Essex v. Warwickshire at Ilford in 1959, was run out by first slip. The wicket-keeper missed a leg-break from W. E. Hollies but A. H. Kardar gathered the ball and hit the stumps with it before Vigar could regain the crease. He was, in effect, stumped by first slip.

☆

Roy Webber also records that at Manchester in 1899, A. Ward, playing for Lancashire against Derbyshire, was given out hit wicket when a ball knocked the shoulder off his bat onto his stumps.

...

During the Surrey v. Sussex game at the Oval in August 1887 the last few Surrey men were told to hit out and get out as quickly as possible. To do this T. Bowley kept running up the pitch to be stumped. The wicket-keeper, W. H. Dudney, refused to accept the stumping chances offered and Bowley was compelled to tread on his wicket deliberately with his score at 22.

At Oxford in 1865 a Mr Wright, playing for Oxford University against the Gentlemen of the Midland Counties, broke his bat while at the wicket so that the shattered blade struck him on the top of the head. From there it fell onto his stumps and he was given out hit wicket.

☆

The Sussex v. Kent match at Brighton in August 1891 revealed yet another way of enlivening the scorebook. C. J. M. Fox, of Kent, apparently dissatisfied with food provided on the ground, went elsewhere for his lunch, returning to discover that the innings had ended and that he was out 'absent'. Benny Green's comment in the index to *Wisden Anthology 1864–1900* was: 'Fox, C. J. M., prefers eating to batting.'

LBW

LBW was first mentioned in the Laws of Cricket in 1774, but the first reference to a batsman being given out lbw occurred in 1795 when the Hon. J. Turton lost his wicket in that manner.

...

Only when an lbw decision involves something extraordinary do the newspapers mention it prominently. In 1923 one batsman in eight was given out lbw and in August the following year, says Gerald Brodribb in his book, *Next Man In*, A. S. Kennedy, the Hampshire all-rounder, was given out that way in six successive innings.

☆

Batsmen in the Ranji Trophy Match betwen Rajputana and Delhi in 1942−43 were even more prone to get their legs in front of their stumps, for seven Rajputanians were given out lbw in their second innings, making a match total of 15 − a record.

...

They would have been happier if Fuller Pilch had been umpiring as he did in his retirement when he was landlord of an inn in Canterbury. Whenever a bowler appealed to him for an lbw decision Pilch always turned it down, saying scornfully, 'Bowl 'em out!'

☆

But batsmen don't need to interpose their legs between ball and stumps to be given out. As C. B. Fry reported in a New Zealand paper during the Test at Sheffield in 1902, G. L. Jessop was given out lbw when a ball from H. Trumble hit him on the top button of his shirt.

...

Tom Pugh, captain of Gloucestershire, made headline news in the match against Northamptonshire at Peterborough in May 1961 when he ducked into a fast ball from David Larter, had his jaw broken in two places and was given out lbw.

In 1932 H. Fisher, the Yorkshire slow left-hander, achieved an lbw hat-trick against Somerset at Sheffield. Similar feats were accomplished by J. A. Flavell for Worcestershire v. Lancashire at Manchester in 1963, M. J. Procter for Gloucestershire v. Essex at Westcliff in 1972 and B. J. Ikin for Griqualand West against Orange Free State at Kimberley in 1973–74.

☆

An article by Peter Roebuck in *The Cricketer* Spring Annual 1981 deals with Norman Teer, who plays for Mendip Acorns and bowls 'donkey-drops'. Apparently 'he launches the ball far into the sky, then relaxes, awaiting the outcome'. In one match the batsman advanced to hit a very high-pitched ball, missed it and saw it roll slowly towards his stumps. At the last moment he rushed back to his crease and stopped the barely moving ball with his foot. 'Norman, keen as ever, appealed for lbw. The umpire ruled in his favour.' The astonished batsman then ran down the wicket, complaining bitterly that 'the ruddy ball wouldn't even have reached the ruddy wicket!'

...

In his first match for South Australia at Adelaide, Sir Donald Bradman was out lbw in both innings for 15 and 50, the *Sunday Times* recalled in May 1981. That was in the 1935–36 season but Bradman enjoyed 45 more innings at Adelaide before being out in the same way. Research showed that in his 295 completed innings the great man was lbw only 27 times – about once every 11 innings. The same paper then analysed the 1980 season in England and discovered that in a total of 4,515 dismissals there were 635 lbw's – a ratio of one in seven.

☆

At Easbourne in 1938 Sussex, playing Gloucestershire, lost all their first six batsmen lbw in knocking up 278.

...

W. G. Grace was dismissed lbw only 54 times in his career in which he batted about 1500 times.

Out on Purpose

Batsmen don't often give their wickets away, but Herbert Sutcliffe did that at Leyton when Yorkshire, playing Essex in 1932, amassed a colossal 555 for the first wicket. Then, convinced that he and his partner, Percy Holmes, had beaten the record previously held by J. T. Brown and J. Tunnicliffe, also of Yorkshire, he allowed himself to be bowled by Eastman. Too late they discovered that they had only equalled the old record 554, but an unrecorded no-ball was found and a new record created.

...

At one stage in his career W. G. Grace, realising that he had scored every amount from 0 to 100 except 93, decided to score just that figure. He had tried for it once and been frustrated by four overthrows but eventually got the coveted figure by lingering on 89 until he struck a four and then gave some grateful bowler a cheap wicket.

☆

While Australia were scoring 721 against Essex at Southend in 1948, Keith Miller told his captain, Bradman, that he didn't want to bat as scoring was too easy. Bradman insisted, so Miller walked to the wicket and when Trevor Bailey bowled his first ball to him, shouldered his bat and didn't make a stroke.

...

During the MCC tour of South Africa in 1956–57 Denis Compton, given not out when he was sure he had been caught in a match against Rhodesia, deliberately gave the simplest catch off the next ball and was walking towards the pavilion before the fielder got a hand to it.

☆

In one Gentlemen v. Players match the story is told of Neville Knox bowling with such venom on a fiery pitch that when one professional arrived at the wicket he withdrew towards square leg as the ball was delivered and allowed it to crash into his stumps. He departed, saying to the fielders, 'Good afternoon, gentlemen, I've got a wife and family to think of.'

When Harold Larwood and Bill Voce were at the height of their considerable powers, Nottinghamshire were playing Leicestershire, one of whose bowlers was wreaking havoc. When Leicester went in to bat they batted circumspectly but Larwood and Voce bowled normally until the successful bowler came in. 'Here he is, Lol,' said a Nottinghamshire player audibly, 'Let him have one.' Larwood obliged with a ball that reared past the newcomer's face. The second was edged towards gully and the batsman started to walk away although there had been no semblance of a catch. 'It was a bump ball. No catch!' gully shouted. Back came the retort: 'Yes it was a catch. I'm quite satisfied.'

...

George Gunn, the famous Nottinghamshire batsman, was quite an eccentric. Once, when told that lunch would be taken an hour later than usual, he gave away his wicket, saying, 'I always have my lunch at one-thirty.' On another occasion he saw his wife arrive to watch the game, deliberately landed a six near her to indicate that he would soon join her and then got himself out.

☆

In May 1900 the Laws of Cricket were altered making the follow-on optional, the margin being increased to 150 for three-day matches. Previously teams had resorted to various methods of making their opponents bat a second time. In 1887, when Nottinghamshire played Surrey at Trent Bridge (*Weekly Telegraph*, 3 June 1939), 'Surrey batsmen deliberately hit their wickets, walked out of their ground to be stumped and wilfully hit catches, in fact did anything to get out. John Shuter was the Surrey captain and his object in ordering these things was to get Notts out and win the match. In that he succeeded.'

Run Out

Frightened out rather than run out should have been the scorebook entry against Pieter Marrish's name in a game at Johannesburg, South Africa, in 1972. He dared not return to his crease because he spotted a snake and the wicket-keeper had plenty of time to whip off the bails.

...

On 2 August 1842 it seems that J. Marshall, playing for Sheffield Iris, lost his wicket 'burnt ball 0'. One or two magazine articles have mentioned this without being able to supply an explanation. There was an equally strange scorebook entry a few years ago when one Stan Dawson, playing at Kalgoorlie, Australia, was hit by a fast delivery that ignited a box of matches in his hip pocket. He was run out as he tried to beat out the flames.

☆

A rare run out decision was given in a match at Blackheath that needs further documentation. An unnamed umpire reminiscing in a popular paper described how Brian Valentine and Jack Davies, batting for Kent, started to run for a shot to cover but 'the ball was fielded so smartly that they knew there was no hope of completing the run. They stopped in the middle of the pitch while the wicket was put down. The question was, which of them was out? They were exactly level and it was impossible to say whether they had crossed. At first each claimed he was not out ... so in the end they tossed for it.'

...

Seven members of the MCC and Ground XI were run out in their match with Sussex at Lord's in August 1860, but the match between Cookley and Bond Worth in the Kidderminster League produced a sequence of run outs that can hardly be beaten. A *Daily Telegraph* writer learned that in July 1966 Bond Worth needed only three runs to win with five wickets down. Off the first ball of the next over a single was scored. 'The next five balls saw the last five Bond Worth batsmen run out, Cookley thus winning by one run.'

Tom Goddard, according to an old friend, was once run out twice in a match without receiving a single ball. Similar misfortune attended R. McLeod in a match between Melbourne and North Melbourne in 1896.

☆

Almost as ludicrous as the Kent run out already mentioned was that involving R. C. Robertson-Glasgow and T. C. Raikes of Somerset in one game against Surrey. Smart fielding left them in the middle of the pitch and both dashed for the same end, beating the ball. They then raced for the other end, again beating the ball. By now, fielders were almost in hysterics. Stumps lay uprooted at both ends, but as the batsmen prepared for their fourth sortie, one fielder, calmer than the rest, picked up the ball and downed a solitary stump. Then, as no one knew who was really out, the batsmen tossed up. Robertson-Glasgow lost and was one of the few men ever to lose his wicket on the spin of a coin.

...

During England's 1911–12 tour of Australia Jack Hobbs ran out 15 men.

☆

H. Charlwood, of Sussex, playing against Surrey at the Oval on one occasion gave a catch to a fielder in the deep and was dropped. He set off for a third run but was dismissed, run out. The second run was signalled 'one short' so that Charlwood was missed, made one run, ran one short and was run out, all from one stroke.

...

In *The Walkers of Southgate* it is stated that V. E. Walker used to follow up his own bowling in the hope of making a caught-and-bowled. In one game he realised that the non-striker was following him up rather closely. So, when the ball was played back to him, he threw it between his legs without turning round and ran out the surprised non-striker.

65

During his schooldays at Eton the Duke of Dorset in 1754 parted
company with his mistress, a lady named Bacelli, after she ran him out
in a cricket match.

☆

At one stage in the Nottinghamshire v. Yorkshire match in 1875
W. Oscroft refused to go when given run out. A conference lasting half
an hour was held in the pavilion before he could be persuaded to give
up his innings.

...

*In 1886 during one Kent match J. W. Foley hit a ball into the crowd.
A spectator picked it up and threw it back. The umpire meanwhile had
signalled four, but a fielder picked up the ball, threw down the wicket
and the batsman was given run out.*

Dress

According to *The Connoisseur*, vol. 9, August 1904, the transition from top hat to cricket cap was not just a whim of fashion. Apparently hats were abolished 'owing to an accident that befell a great batsman'. He had been batting some time and seemed set for a good score when his topper fell onto his stumps and he was given out. 'For a while there was an interesting inconsequence about cricket hats. Old prints show players in all sorts and conditions of head-gear, from the original round ''Zingari'' cap to a cumbersome article of the gold style. Only quite recently was the cricket cap we all know so well introduced.'

...

In 1939 a cricket correspondent reported that members of Churt (Surrey) second XI were such poor fielders that anyone dropping a catch had to wear a special red hat until the next one was missed. Even if anyone wearing the red hat redeemed the situation by holding a blinder or two he was not allowed to discard it until the next catch was dropped.

☆

The first English cricketers to visit Australia (1861–62) wore distinguishing colours so that spectators could identify them by referring to their match cards. Every man wore a light helmet and sash, each of a different colour.

...

On 4 July 1972 the *Daily Mirror* mentioned that Chelston CC at Torbay, Devon, had equipped their wicket-keeper with lemon and black gloves. Their batsmen took the field in blue and yellow striped pads. 'Worse still, the club is trying to get matching shirts.'

An article in the *Strand Magazine* for 1895 stated that members of the old Hambledon team wore breeches, stockings, buckled shoes and velvet caps. Lord Winchelsea's team used to wear silver-laced caps.

☆

In the match between Middlesex and Gloucestershire at Clifton in 1860 it is said that Alfred Lyttelton kept wicket wearing a hard straw hat.

...

Many cricket writers agree that the umpire's white coat was first donned in a match between the Free Foresters and the United England XI at Eccles, Lancashire, in 1861. The Rev. W. G. Armitstead protested that he could not see the bowler's arm against the dark background of the umpire's body. An old-fashioned nightshirt was found and the umpire wore that for the rest of the game.

☆

An article of cricket clothing, not intended for cricketers, was seen on sale in a London shop in August 1961 by an alert reporter. It was a Rain Stopped Play tie and the motif on it was, very aptly, an opened umbrella over three cricket stumps.

...

In 1870 George Summers, of Nottinghamshire, was knocked out when a ball from George Freeman, the Yorkshire fast bowler, hit him on the cheekbone and he died three days later. The next man in, Richard Daft, arrived at the wicket with his head swathed in towels as if he were wearing an enormous turban.

☆

Derbyshire players fielded in their ordinary clothes at one time during their match against Yorkshire at Dewsbury in 1899. Heavy rain had flooded their dressing room. The only two players unaffected, Wright and Higson, had spiked shoes and had to bowl.

Ducks

Various publications list the five players who have the greatest number of consecutive ducks – nine – to their names. They are T. W. J. Goddard (Gloucestershire) in 1923; A. H. S. Clark (Somerset) in 1930, his nine innings being a complete record of his career in county cricket; O. S. Wheatley (Glamorganshire) in 1966; B. S. Boshier (Leicestershire) in 1955 and M. W. Selvey (Middlesex) in 1972. Some of the ducks were 0 not out and in some cases enabled other batsmen to score valuable runs. Boshier's sequence was broken when he was top scorer in his next match with 13 runs against Lancashire.

…

Cricket statistician Irving Rosenwater has stated that Arthur Morris (Australia) played his first hundred innings before being dismissed without scoring; he also mentions that J. T. Ikin (Lancashire) did not collect his first duck in England until he had batted a hundred times. His first duck came at Brisbane (1946–47) in the Test and was his fifty-seventh first-class innings.

☆

Sir Donald Bradman made only 16 ducks in first-class games – more than any other individual score against his name. He made seven in Tests, Rosenwater notes, and in his last innings was bowled by Eric Hollies, second ball, without scoring.

…

A brief note in a daily paper for 19 July 1958 informed us that Jack D'Arcy, the New Zealand opener, took 53 minutes to score his duck at Lord's the previous day.

☆

In his biography of Patsy Hendren, I. A. R. Peebles mentioned that the old Middlesex stalwart collected ducks in his first and last first-class innings. In between, however, he scored 56,611 runs, including 170 centuries.

In the obituary of S. S. Schultz, who died in 1937, *Wisden* recalled that he once played on the Christ Church ground in 1881 and the pitch was so bumpy that the Gentlemen of England, intimidated by the success of some unnamed fast bowler, refused to play on. The match was re-started in The Parks and Schultz, out first ball at Christ Church, was given another chance in The Parks, but was again out first ball – two ducks in one innings.

...

In 1862 C. Absolon, bowling underarm against XX of the Metropolitan CC, bowled 18 of them. Their innings totalled 4, including 18 ducks. (Roy Webber, *Cricket Records*.)

☆

On one occasion, to quote Irving Rosenwater, 'Three ducks in a single match was the fate of both W. Welsh and W. Richmond, playing for XIII of Bingham v. Nottingham Old Club at Bingham in 1834, when the arrangement was that the Bingham team should have four innings to Nottingham's two.'

...

According to *The Cricketer* for September 1980, one Joseph Emile Patrick McMaster toured South Africa with Major Warton's 1888–89 team. He batted at no. 9, made a duck and did not bowl. That was his only first-class game.

☆

The record for the quickest 'pair' – a duck in each innings – was achieved by Peter Judge, of Glamorgan, last man in against India at Cardiff. He was bowled first ball by Sarwate and, to save time when the county followed on, Judge and J. C. Clay stayed on the field to open the second innings. Sarwate clean bowled Judge again, first ball.

...

George Hirst, Yorkshire, collected more ducks – 106 – than any other leading batsman.

Walter Hammond and Phillip Mead both collected three 'pairs' in their long careers, but W. G. Grace, Ranji, Sir Jack Hobbs, Sir Donald Bradman and Denis Compton never registered pairs.

☆

An alert reporter at Lord's on 7 August 1955 covering the Combined Services v. Public Schools match noted this scorebook entry: Shirreff b. Duck 0. And another newsman noted a local match at Burnham, Essex, in which two batsmen, C. Duck and S. Duck, were each out for ducks.

...

Many minor teams have been dismissed without any batsman scoring. On 22 June 1952 at Bookham, Surrey, the local club dismissed the Electrical Trades Commercial Travellers Association CC for a total of 0 and the game was won without a run being scored from the bat. The first ball in Bookham's innings went for four byes.

☆

'In four overs and 20 minutes the entire Ross County cricket team was dismissed for a duck at Elgin at the weekend in a North of Scotland League game.'

Daily paper report on 1 June 1964

...

The *Daily Mirror* reported on 25 May 1964 that the all-male team of Martin Walter Ltd, a firm of vehicle-builders in Folkestone, Kent, had been skittled out for 0 after 23 minutes, eight maiden overs and two balls. So 28-year-old Mrs Jean de Vere, at various times scorer, secretary and umpire to the scoreless XI, said that she would take over as coach if her husband would baby-sit while she supervised net practice.

☆

In the early 1920s J. Martison, opening bat for Eastrington, near Selby, Yorkshire, carried his bat out for 0 when a Mr Tune, for Cliffe Common, took all ten wickets for no runs.

From press reports it seems that at least three county sides had 'baggers' ties' which were obligatory wear for those unfortunates who bagged a pair. The Essex tie was a yellow confection decorated with two red ducks and two white haloes. 'It's hideous' was one player's comment, but he had to wear it before play on the first morning of each match or buy a round of drinks as a forfeit. Ray Smith of Essex in the late 1950s was burdened with his tie for 15 months. Freddie Stocks, of Nottinghamshire, was simultaneously wearing one, but it passed next, and surprisingly, to Reg Simpson, who 'qualified' against Warwickshire a week later. Hampshire players also have a baggers' tie.

...

A previous report (20 August 1955) stated that Trevor Bailey, of Essex and England, was sporting a tie emblazoned with a red duck inside a circle. It was, he said, the tie of the 'Bloody Duck' Club. 'An ordinary duck won't do. Mine was at Sydney and it took me 45 minutes.'

☆

In less exalted circles Bungay CC, Suffolk, instituted their version of the non-scorer's tie. It was navy blue with an embroidered duck on it. Anyone making a duck had to wear it until the next duck was registered. The skipper who awarded it to his scoreless men had a busy time on the tie's first airing. Six members of the side failed to score.

...

On 28 December 1954 it was reported that cricket had been played on Boxing Day at Chedworth, Gloucestershire. The home team lost to visitors from Cheltenham and Mr C. E. Baker was presented with a dead duck to mark the fact that he was the first batsman failing to score.

☆

On 27 July 1960 film star Trevor Howard rose at 5 am and travelled 180 miles to play cricket at Buxton, Derbyshire, only to be out first ball, caught at the wicket.

...

Sir Len Hutton scored three consecutive ducks in June 1949, one in a Test and the next two against Worcestershire. But that didn't stop him from amassing 1,294 runs in that same June – still a record for a month's cricket.

Early Starts

To celebrate their one hundred and twenty-fifth anniversary on 17 May 1961, Tring Park CC's players left their homes in the middle of the night and started playing at 5 am. They breakfasted when the game ended and then went off to work.

...

That was just a 'one-off' fixture, but years ago a number of clubs thought nothing of playing cricket regularly as dawn broke, usually for practice. In Yorkshire – where else? – members of York CC in 1784 drew up a set of rules by which the 31 signatories agreed to meet on Heworth Moor every Tuesday and Friday morning at 4 am until 5 September 'for the purpose of playing at Cricket, to play for one Penny a Game, and to Fine Three Pence if not within sight of the wickets before the Minster strikes five o'clock.' Players subscribed a shilling each and this, plus the fines, paid for a club dinner at the end of the season.

☆

The Hastings Priory CC was formed in 1856 and members agreed that, because of the difficulty in getting time off, they should practise every Monday, Wednesday and Friday at 5.30 am on West Hill. On one occasion at least they played a match at that hour against the East End Amateur Club, play ending to give the players time to get to work. The match was so popular that their employers arranged a return game on a Tuesday afternoon.

...

Humour in Sports by John Aye quotes a poster as follows: 'Novel Match. A Cricket Match between the Upper Mitcham Early Rising Association versus Lower Mitcham Peep o' Day Club will be played on Lower Mitcham Green on Wednesday mornings July 6th. and 13th., 1870. Wickets will be pitched at 3.30 a.m. Play to commence at 4 precisely. Stumps to be drawn at 7 o'clock each morning.'

FANTASTIC BUTLER, JEEVES. HIT 197 BEFORE BREKKER YESTERDAY

A few years ago Mr G. J. Morphy of Rye, Sussex, discovered the 'articles of the Rye Morning Dew Cricket Club', dated 1849. According to these 'every Monday, Wednesday and Friday mornings (weather permitting) the members shall meet on the Town Salts and any member not present at fifteen minutes past 5 o'clock shall forfeit 2d.' If he had no reasonable excuse for being late he was fined 4d. Umpires, presumably, were not so keen on early-morning matches, for the Rye men agreed that the decision of a batsman being out rested, not with an umpire, but with the majority of the players present. One odd rule barred any member from hitting his wicket with the flat of his bat under penalty of a 6d fine. Other fines must have been imposed for other offences as anyone refusing to pay the fines was automatically expelled.

☆

The Early Bird CC, founded in 1897, was rather different. Its members were gentlemen's gentlemen and servants recruited from the big houses in London's fashionable quarters. Butlers, valets, footmen and others were allowed to use Battersea Park playing fields every Tuesday and they started practising at 5.30 am so that the players could hurry back home in time to arouse their employers. Practice must have been beneficial for a few years later they were playing crack-of-dawn matches against a number of similar early risers. Later on they played against sides made up from staffs on country estates and in 1939 the Early Birds became a wandering club. Two years later they recruited some guardsmen who were on leave or otherwise available and once played at Lord's against the Metropolitan Police.

Extras

Wisden's obituary of the Rev. Richard Harold Fowler, who died on 27 October 1970, stated that he 'played a few matches for Worcestershire in 1921, took 5 for 33 v. Gloucestershire at Stourbridge, and later was told that only his Cloth saved him from being no-balled; this doubtless accounted for the brevity of his first-class career.'

...

Cambridge University's innings v. Oxford University in 1839 amounted to 287 which included 24 byes and 46 wides. 'The bowlers evidently at times lost their tempers at not being enabled to disturb the wickets of their opponents,' goes a contemporary report.

☆

On 22 August 1955 the greatest number of extras was conceded in a first-class innings: 73 in the Northants v. Kent game at Northampton. Tony Catt, Kent's no.3 wicket-keeper, conceded 48 byes, 11 of them fours. 23 leg-byes and two wides were further welcome additions to the Northamptonshire total.

...

Four byes *in front* of the batsman were achieved in the Roses match in August 1963. Grieves, of Lancashire, allowed a ball from Close to go down the leg side. Binks, the wicket-keeper, diverted it to Trueman whose attempt to return it to the bowler sent it over mid-on's head to the long-on boundary. After a consultation the umpires decided that the ball was not dead when the wicket-keeper touched it and the four was recorded as byes.

Fielding

On MCC's 1962–63 tour of Australia the Rev. David Sheppard, as he then was, had an unhappy time in the field, missed chances off Freddie Trueman, and eventually was sent out to fine leg, out of the way. Then Bill Lawry hooked a ball towards him and David brought off a wonderful running catch, low down. As he acknowledged the plaudits of the crowd, holding up the ball for all to see, Fred Titmus panted up. 'David,' he said, 'will you throw the ball in or shall I? It was a no-ball and they've already run five.'

...

Playing for Nottinghamshire against Hampshire in 1913 G. M. Lee caught all the first five Hampshire batsmen.

☆

Years ago – and maybe still today – a cricket club at Radcliffe, Lancashire, employed a useful extra fielder. Next to the ground was a reservoir into which the big hitters sometimes lofted a ball. The treasurer did not worry about balls lost there. A well-trained dog was stationed handily so that he could jump into the water and retrieve the ball.

...

Another club to have a four-footed fielder was Billeston CC in Leicestershire. For ten years, said a newspaper report in July 1964, the club was assisted by Bonzo, a spaniel, who had been trained to field at third man, not to prevent runs but to retrieve balls hit into some undergrowth. In eleven years on duty Bonzo had not lost a single ball.

☆

A. C. Williams, acting as twelfth man for Leicestershire v. Yorkshire at Huddersfield in 1919, was a Yorkshire player and caught out four members of his own team.

A highly respected and useful member of the famous Grace family, says the *Dictionary of Extra-ordinary English Cricketers*, was Ponto, 'the bravest of the Grace family's dogs'. He was an expert fielder, often stopping hard-hit balls with his chest and retrieving the ball from an orchard, having apparently judged its course by the noise it made among the crashing branches.

...

Long stop was once a recognised fielding position, but in 1873 H. Phillips, the Sussex wicket-keeper, was so effective that in Gloucestershire's second innings no long stop was used.

☆

Once, during a visit to Australia, W. G. Grace was greatly impressed by the fielding of a small boy. He insisted that the youngster should also demonstrate his batting skill — if any — and when the boy had spent some time in the nets, Grace said, 'You can field, my lad, but I'm afraid you'll never make a batsman.' The boy was Victor Trumper.

...

Peter Walker, the Glamorgan and England player, attributed his fielding skill to a journey on a cargo boat which he took as a youth. He and a young seaman whiled away the time throwing potatoes at each other across the deck, with severe penalties for any that were allowed to slip overboard.

First Facts

There is some confusion about who scored the first recorded century. *Wisden* states that Minshull's 107 for the Duke of Dorset's XI v. Wrotham, Kent, in 1769 was the earliest. Roy Webber's *Cricket Records* credits John Small jnr's 108 for Hambledon v. Surrey at Hambledon in 1774 as the first. Both agree, however, that the first man to score a century in each innings of a match was W. Lambert who did so for Sussex v. Epsom at Lord's in 1817. The first recorded double century was scored by William Ward for MCC when he knocked up 278 against Norfolk at Lord's in 1820.

...

MCC's first match outside Britain was played in Paris on 22–23 April 1867.

☆

The telegraph scoreboard was first used at Lord's in 1846, the year in which scorecards were first sold there.

...

The first important match for which the full score was preserved was played in 1744 on the Artillery Ground, Finsbury, between Kent and All-England, Kent winning by one wicket.

☆

The first record of a cricket match played outside England was a match at Aleppo in 1676 between the Navy and British Residents.

The first match played by an English team overseas took place in Montreal in 1859 when XI of England met XXII of Lower Canada. In the same year the first international cricket match was played at Hoboken, New York, between XI of England and XXII of USA. (*Gillette Book of Cricket and Football*.)

...

England's first team to visit Australia sailed from Liverpool on 20 October 1861 in the *Great Britain*. The voyage lasted 65 days and the players were paid £150 each, plus expenses. This was a business speculation and was arranged by Messrs Spiers and Pond, a catering firm.

Gifts

When L. Amarnath scored 118 against England at Bombay in 1933–34 it was the first century for India in a Test. Spectators were so delighted that Hindu women tore off their jewels and showered them on him as presents. A millionaire gave him £800 and another presented him with a car.

...

The first Pakistani batsman to score a hundred in a Test was 19-year-old Hanif Mohammad who knocked up 142 against India at Bahawalpur in January 1955. A local business man was so delighted that he presented him with 2,000 rupees – £150.

☆

Maurice Leyland in May 1958 offered to give Freddie Trueman a stone of mint humbugs if he scored 50 in the match against Hampshire at Bradford. Freddie obliged with a whirlwind 58 in 27 minutes and Leyland then went on a Yorkshire-wide search for bags of humbugs.

...

While playing for his native Natal in a Currie Cup match in 1971, Barry Richards was offered £1 for every run he scored. Almost immediately he earned, and was paid, £167 for 167 runs. While playing in Australia in the previous year he received one Australian dollar for every run he scored. His total for the period was 1,538 runs which worked out at about £722.

☆

For scoring 105 in the second Test against South Africa in September 1965 at Nottingham, Colin Cowdrey won 100 bottles of wines, spirits and liqueurs offered by a South African organisation.

Every four hit in the MCC v. Victoria Country XI at Shepparton in December 1962 earned the batsman a pair of socks. Each six was rewarded with a case of fruit. MCC won two cases of fruit and 22 pairs of socks.

...

Sir Don Bradman's 334 v. England at Leeds in 1930 brought him a cheque for £1,000 from a wealthy Australian businessman.

☆

When Jim Laker took 19 wickets against Australia at Manchester in 1956 he was given £190 – £10 for each wicket – by the printing firm, Thomas De La Rue.

Grounds

No wonder Worcester cricket ground was Sir Donald Bradman's favourite. On his first visit in 1930 he scored 236 against the county. In 1934 he scored 206, 258 in 1938 and 107 in 1948, thus scoring a total of 807 runs for an average of 201.75.

...

Almost every year the Worcester ground is under water when the River Severn, which runs past it, overflows. In 1934 a 45 lb salmon was caught by the head groundsman who spotted it thrashing about near the grandstand, caught it in a cricket net and sold it to a local fishmonger. On another occasion the iron roller floated away and was only saved when the shafts caught in an iron fence. In 1924 a grand piano floated over the ground; it had been washed away from the fair held on Worcester racecourse. In one severe storm the Rev. G. W. Gillingham, the club's honorary secretary, actually swam to the office to rescue tickets for an important match which had to be switched to another less watery venue.

☆

One of the smallest grounds used for cricket was probably that at Kyleakin on the Isle of Skye. It was the only level patch of ground for 50 miles round and was little bigger than a full-sized tennis court. So the striker was always at the same end, the on-side boundary was the sea and fielders were posted in the heather, on mountain-sides and even in shallow water on the shore of the loch. At one time, if not nowadays, matches were played between local enthusiasts and teams from visiting Coast Line steamers. A letter in *The Cricketer* for 11 June 1950 from a correspondent who had taken part in one game at Kyleakin stated that originally the matches were played on the mainland in Kyle but, when that pitch was built over during the second world war, the games were resumed at Kyleakin although 'it was expected that the new ground at Kyle would be put into use in 1954'.

Another cricket ground of unusual dimensions was used by Schiedam CC, Holland, for 75 years until 1960. The pitch was narrower than it was long, the wicket was pitched diagonally across it and bowling was always from the same end. When 'over' was called both batsmen and umpires changed ends.

...

In 1844 the Oval was a market garden, in danger of being built on. Happily the Montpelier Club lost its ground in Southwark and persuaded the Otter Trustees, who had leased the land from the Duchy of Cornwall, to let them take it over and convert it into a 'Subscription Cricket Ground'. The lease described the land as 'in a most ruinous condition and from the effluvium arising from the decayed vegetables, a nuisance and a source of ill health'. A pitch was laid with 10,000 turves from Tooting Common and in 1845 the first match was played there between the Gentlemen and Players of Surrey.

Six years later the builders again threatened another invasion but the Prince Consort, acting for the Prince of Wales (who was also the Duke of Cornwall and later became King Edward VII), intervened and the Oval was saved for cricket. The ground, at first shared by the Montpelier and Surrey Clubs, later reverted to Surrey CCC which, though it ultimately flourished, faced more difficulties.

Plans to build a pub were cancelled because of complaints from nearby householders of rowdyism. Meanwhile the Oval was being used for a variety of non-cricketing purposes. In 1851 a walking match of 1,000 miles in 1,000 hours was organised by William Houghton, the lessee. He suggested a poultry exhibition for New Year's Day 1853 but the Duchy banned that. In 1875 the Club bought the remainder of the lease which decreed that 'no game or sport other than the game of cricket, football, tennis, fives, rackets and amateur athletic sports shall be played' at the Oval. However, permission to construct an asphalt skating rink was granted and it was used for a while. Tennis, hockey, Rugby and soccer were all played at the Oval and the FA Cup Finals were played there from 1872 to 1892.

The first Test match between England and Australia in England was played at the Oval on 6, 7, and 8 September 1880 when Surrey CCC's secretary, C. W. Alcock, helped the visitors, who had arrived without having organised any fixtures and were reduced to advertising to get matches, by arranging it. More than 40,000 watched play.

Several matches have been played on the Goodwin Sands and, judging from an old print, crews of the *Hecla* and *Fury* played on the ice near Igooli, near the seventieth parallel, in 1823. The players are shown clad in furs with their ships locked in the ice-field a mile or so away.

☆

When the *Great Eastern*, the biggest ship of her time, was lying in Southampton Water soon after her launch in 1859 and before she was due to set sail on her maiden Atlantic voyage, a cricket match was played aboard her. The ship proved to be a costly flop and its owners, glad to raise money in any way, arranged it. Apparently the ball never went overboard during the game which suggests that, despite the ship's size, the batsmen were by no means big hitters.

Interruptions

At Howick, near Pietermaritzburg, South Africa, in March 1958 a match was held up by the wife of one of the players telephoning him while he was at the wicket. She wanted to know what he had done with the soap.

...

Lancashire's second innings in a match against Leicestershire at Nelson was once brought to an unexpected halt by Eckersley, the home captain. He was batting when he heard a bell sound and, assuming that it was a signal from the county committee to close the innings, declared. The committee thought that was his decision. In fact the bell had been rung in a nearby street by a man selling muffins.

☆

The Middlesex v. Hampshire match at Lord's on 19 July 1956 was held up while umpires asked that a light in the pavilion should be switched off. It had been troubling the batsmen.

...

The start of the Middlesex second innings in their match against Sussex at Hove was delayed on 2 August 1954 while an iron pipe was dug out of the pitch. It was found embedded in one of the creases. No-one could discover how it had got there.

☆

Play in the Yorkshire v. MCC match at Scarborough on 9 September 1961 was suspended when Colin Ingleby-Mackenzie was discovered on the boundary listening to a radio broadcast of the St Leger, quite oblivious of the game. From one of his gestures, a 'thumbs down' sign, his team-mates gathered that he had backed a loser.

The second day of the Jubilee Test between India and England in February 1980 was declared a rest day when it was realised that an eclipse of the sun was due that afternoon. The Indian Board, in agreement with the English team, said the *Daily Telegraph*, did not want the responsibility of a crowd of 50,000 damaging their eyes looking into the sun as the moon partially obscured it.

...

After only one ball had been bowled the match between a mixed team of Fijians and Europeans under the Hon. J. A. Udal in 1906 on the island of Taveuni was abandoned. It dismissed the High Chief and he was so displeased that it was thought wiser to proceed no further.

☆

An apple stopped play for a while in the Pakistan v. Glamorgan match at Swansea on 1 August 1954. One batsman, Wazir Mohammad, was inconvenienced when the sun flashed on the knife used by a spectator to peel the fruit. He resumed when the nuisance had been stopped.

...

Rain stopped play in the India v. Worcestershire match at Worcester on 4 May 1967, reported the *Daily Mirror*. After batting for about ten minutes F. M. Engineer appealed to the opposing captain, Don Kenyon, to have play suspended because of the rain. 'This isn't a light appeal,' he pointed out, 'but the rain is getting in my eyes.'

☆

Play was stopped for a few moments at Bramall Lane, Sheffield, on 10 July 1953 when Yorkshire were playing Gloucestershire. Pieces of ice, some six inches square, fell onto the pitch, it was presumed from a high-flying aeroplane.

The scorebook of the Aden-based Venturers CC recorded on 10 August 1967: 'Play delayed 10 minutes by mortar attack.'

...

In July 1893, wrote R. Roberts in *Sixty Years of Somerset Cricket*, the Australians in Taunton to play Somerset realised that the pitch had been badly affected by rain. By some misunderstanding they thought play was off for the day and therefore set off in a large horse-brake for a picnic, but about 2 pm the umpires, after an inspection, decided that play was now possible. Telegrams and messengers were sent to contact the missing players who returned about 4 pm and the match was resumed.

Unusual Matches

Robert Graves in *Goodbye to All That* recorded on 24 June 1915: 'Vermelles. This afternoon we had a cricket match, officers versus sergeants, in an enclosure between some houses out of observation of the enemy. Our front line is perhaps three-quarters of a mile away. I made top score, 24; the bat was a bit of rafter, the ball a piece of rag tied round with string and the wicket a parrot cage with the clean dry corpse of a parrot inside. It had evidently died of starvation when the French evacuated the town. Machine-gun fire broke up the match.'

...

Perhaps the strangest cricket match on record was that played on the stage of the Coliseum Theatre, London, in February 1908 between Surrey and Middlesex. Four Middlesex men were captained by Albert Trott, while Surrey's quartet was not quoted in *The House that Stoll Built* by Felix Barker in his description of the game. Stumps were 15 yards apart and play went on against a backcloth showing a tree-fringed ground. A net protected the audience from full-blooded hits but at one performance it could not be used and the game went on without it, the stalls being bombarded as a four-ounce ball, driven by lightweight bats, kept the audience busy. At least one run had to be tried for every hit and runs were accumulated from one show to the next. The audience was provided with scorecards and an official scorer lurked in the wings. By Wednesday Middlesex were leading by 136 runs to 125 and scores were neck and neck until the final day, Saturday. A cup had been promised to the winners but towards the end it was realised that it had not been bought. The players, who had been paid only £5 each for the week's play, suspected meanness on the management's part and the winners, Middlesex, were presented with a hastily polished tankard from a nearby pub.

A match played over 24 consecutive hours and starting at 5 pm was played on Parker's Piece, Cambridge, in June 1973. One batsman, Roger Coates, reading history at Christ's, scored a century, his innings starting at 1.43 am and including 14 boundaries. The usual intervals were observed, including a break of 30 minutes for breakfast which was served at Emmanuel College. At the end the two teams had scored between them 1,395 runs from 367 overs in ten innings. During the hours of darkness the main source of light was four street lights and two gas arc-lamps placed at extra-cover and mid-wicket. Fast bowling was banned during the darkest hours and spectators included for a while the New Zealand Test team but dwindled to three under-graduates at 2 am. When they disappeared the game was watched by one youth on a bicycle. A collection was taken, to which the New Zealanders contributed generously, and raised £150 for the mentally handicapped.

☆

Two teams mounted on horses played cricket at Bromley, Kent, on 30 July 1735. They were recruited by the Earl of Middlesex and Prince Frederick, son of George II, for a stake of £1,000. Middlesex, batting first, scored 72 and Kent replied with 95. Middlesex at the second attempt scored only 32 and Kent won easily. A similar match between teams mounted on ponies took place at Harrietsham, Kent, in 1800. In this the players used specially made, long-handled bats.

...

At Hove on several occasions matches have been played between teams dressed in Regency clothes and using bats of the style in vogue about 1820.

☆

In 1796 a team of Greenwich Pensioners, each with only one leg, played a team each of whom had only one arm, at Walworth before a great crowd. The one-legged men won by 111 runs (the complete scores not having been preserved apparently). There were five casualties, all broken legs – wooden ones. One was broken by a blow from a bat while the others were broken in running.

Cricket was once played on stilts in Kent between teams of hop-pickers, using hop-poles as stumps. The bats were small squares of wood tied to broom handles.

...

In 1867 at Plymouth the team of Ugly Men played the Handsome Men, the result being a draw. That seems to have started a craze for choosing elevens of all sorts. Right-Handers played Left-Handers at Lord's on 9 and 10 May 1870 and a Married v. Single match played at Lord's on 10 and 12 July 1871 gave W. G. Grace the opportunity of scoring an unbeaten 189. May 1892 saw another Married v. Single match at Lord's for the benefit of Robert Clayton, a Yorkshireman on MCC's ground staff. In addition to North v. South there have been East v. West matches and teams made up of men whose surnames began with the letters A to L against the M to Z brigade.

COME ON, JEKYLL..WHOSE SIDE ARE YOU ON?

In India in 1894 a team of Indians using orthodox bats played a side of Army officers batting with umbrellas.

. . .

Until 7 July 1976 the longest cricket match on record had been played in Australia and had lasted 48 hours and 7 minutes. This was surpassed at Edmonton when the Eccentrics met the Egocentrics in a game scheduled to last 52 hours. It was briefly reported in the *Evening News* which stated that 3,051 runs had been scored for the loss of 150 wickets. One player who sustained a broken finger continued to play with his injured arm in a sling and brought off 'a marvellous left-handed catch to dismiss the batsman who had earlier injured him'.

☆

A match between 'Sixteen of the Country round Sheffield v. Sixteen of Sheffield', played on the Hyde Park Ground on 13 August 1838, was remarkable for the fact that all the players were at least 60 years old.

Music and Cricket

Colin Blythe, the Kent and England left-arm slow bowler, who was killed in action in November 1917, was a talented violinist.

...

While waiting for the next batsman to reach the wicket, George Leer, an eighteenth-century Hambledon cricketer, whiled away the time by singing glees in a high alto voice with the wicket-keeper, a tenor.

☆

John Small sr, born in Empshott, near Petersfield, Hampshire, in 1737, after gaining a one-wicket victory over his great rival, Lumpy Stevens, was presented by the Duke of Dorset with a fine violin. In return Small made two cricket bats and presented them to the duke. He also played the double bass and one day while returning home with his instrument from a musical party was faced by an angry bull as he crossed a field. Unperturbed, Small played a tune on his bass, pacified the animal and reached home unscathed.

Ordered Off

Ordering a player off the field is a common enough feature of football. The Laws of Cricket do not mention such a proceeding, yet on several occasions players have been told to return to the pavilion and stay there. Tony Lock, when playing in a Sheffield Shield match in Australia in November 1964, was sent off – but not for any offence or unsporting action. He was told to wash from his spinning finger the Friar's Balsam many bowlers use to toughen the skin.

. . .

During the Derbyshire v. Yorkshire match at Chesterfield on 18 June 1973 the *Daily Telegraph* reported that Alan Ward, the Derbyshire and England fast bowler, was sent from the field by his captain, Brian Bolus, apparently for refusing to bowl.

☆

Equally remarkable was the incident in which Jack Newman, the veteran Hampshire all-rounder, was involved at Trent Bridge in a game against Nottinghamshire. Newman lost his temper over an umpire's decision and in his frustration kicked the stumps down. His captain, Lord Tennyson, ordered him off and at close of play sent for Newman and the two sat alone in the amateurs' room. Under Tennyson's direction the professional wrote three identical letters, to the President of Nottinghamshire CCC, to A. W. Carr, the Nottinghamshire captain, and to Tennyson himself, stating: 'Dear..., I humbly apologise for my action on the field of play at Trent Bridge and herewith I tender my deep regret. Signed Jack Newman.' Then Lord Tennyson said, 'Don't misbehave yourself again – and here's a fiver for you, you ruddy idiot!'

. . .

In effect the entire Hyderabad team was sent off or sacked, said a note in *Wisden Cricket Monthly* in January 1981, on the eve of their match against Mafatlal at Moin-ud-Dowlah. They had stayed away from an official lunch as a protest in support of their captain, Narasimha Rao, who had been reprimanded for wearing a track-suit at practice. Hyderabad CA substituted an entirely fresh team which lost by an innings and 150 runs.

Relatives

Brothers have often appeared in first-class cricket, often on the same side, but sometimes in opposing teams. Much more unusual are instances of fathers and sons playing together. George Gunn junior was never as famous as his father George, who played his last game for England when he was 49 years old. The two Georges provide the only case of both father and son scoring centuries in the same innings of a county match – for Nottinghamshire against Warwickshire in 1931.

...

The match between Kent and Northamptonshire at Northampton in 1913 was remarkable for the appearance of two pairs of brothers, Frank Woolley and James Seymour appeared for Kent and their brothers, Claude Woolley and John Seymour, played for the home side. This oddity was repeated when the two sides met again at Dover.

☆

A scorebook oddity resulted from the Northamptonshire v. Sussex match in June 1965, in Northampton's first innings:

> Watts, P. J. c. Parks b. Oakman, 13.
> Watts, P. D. c. Parks b. Oakman, 13.

Peter David Watts and Patrick James Watts were brothers, but not twins.

...

In the 1919 University match two sets of brothers were opposed, wrote Roy Webber in his *Cricket Records*. A. E. R. Gilligan and J. H. Naumann played for Cambridge University while F. W. Gilligan and F. C. G. Naumann played for Oxford University.

Father and son batted to the bowling of father and son when Derbyshire met Warwickshire at Derby in 1922. W. G. and B. W. Quaife batted to the bowling of W. and R. Bestwick.

☆

During the MCC tour of Pakistan there were two players named Khalid Aziz in the North Zone team which played the tourists in February 1967. In their first innings both these men were dismissed in the same way: c. Brearley b. Hobbs.

...

Matches between family teams – the Edriches are a notable example – are fairly common. One played at Shrewsbury on 6 August 1967 was reported in several newspapers although no prominent cricketers were concerned. A team of Joneses faced the Shrewsbury first XI and skipper Richard Jones made the scorer's job easier by shouting the Christian name of each bowler to the scorebox. The scorer was called Jones. So was one of the umpires and tea was served by a team of ladies called Mrs Jones or Miss Jones, plus a few single ladies who hoped to become Mrs Jones eventually.

☆

HH Bhagwat Sinhji, Maharana of Mewar, and his son, Yuvraj Arvind Kumar Singh, both played for Rajasthan against Vidarbha at Udaipur in the 1961–62 Ranji Trophy.

...

The case of M. G. Vijayasarathy and M. V. Nagendra, umpires in the Ranji Trophy match between Mysore and Andhra at Bangalore in 1960–61, is unique. Despite their different names, Bill Frindall in *The Kaye Book of Cricket Records* states that they were father and son.

☆

Alec and Eric Bedser of Surrey are not the only twins to have played first-class cricket. J. S. and W. H. Denton played for Northamptonshire, A. D. E. and A. W. S. Rippon for Somerset and F. G. and W. H. Stephens for Warwickshire.

Royalty and Cricket

The member of the Royal Family best known for his association with cricket was undoubtedly Prince Frederick Louis of Wales, who died in 1751. A small man, he does not seem to have been very expert at the game, but he was very fond of it and practised keenly at Cliveden House, his Buckinghamshire home. It was there that he was hit on the side by a cricket ball and died from internal injuries caused by it. So a cricket ball changed the course of history. Instead of King Frederick I, George III came to the throne.

...

On 28 June 1924 *John O' London's Weekly* told how another member of the Royal Family figured in a cricket match. HRH the Prince of Wales, b. Wright, 0 was the scorebook entry in a game played at Sandringham on 17 July 1866. The occasion was a match between the Gentlemen of Norwich and I Zingari. 'A lob bowler took the Prince's wicket. In the field he gave a satisfactory account of himself at short-leg. HRH was playing for I Zingari who registered an easy victory by an innings and 38 runs.'

☆

The Prince, eventually His Majesty King Edward VII, was keen enough to engage William Chatterton, who once did the double for Derbyshire, as his coach. Whatever the King's capabilities the old professional 'could make nothing of 'em', referring to the Royal Children.

...

When George IV was still Prince of Wales he was sufficiently interested in the game to open the Brighton ground in 1792 when Brighton was still a small fishing village. To celebrate the event the locals played the MCC and apparently the match could not be finished in three days, so it was continued on 27 May in the following year.

The Prince was a keen player, took part in many matches and considered himself one of the best batsmen in the land! He happened to hear of a shoemaker from Slough who was reputed to have a strong arm and a keen eye and had accomplished many impressive feats. So the cobbler was invited to play in a match between Bedfordshire and Buckinghamshire in which the Prince played disguised as a civilian. A contemporary report said: 'It soon fell to his Royal Highness to take the bat. ''What bit of a thing is that at the wicket?'' said the cobbler. ''Oh, he is a tailor,'' said someone who stood by. ''Then,'' said the bowler, ''I'll break his bat for him.'' He took his run and sent the ball with amazing force and velocity. The Prince blocked it dead as stone.'

The cobbler bowled many deliveries from which the Prince scored some runs. Then the bowler 'went back to a considerable distance, took an exact aim, ran with all his force to the popping crease – and gently as thistledown flies along the air, the ball ran along the grass like a snake and stopped just in the middle of the wicket, knocking off the crosspiece.'

The Prince, exasperated, threw down his bat. Then he walked to the cobbler, put a heavy purse in his hand and left the field. Next morning the cobbler received an invitation to attend Windsor Castle. 'If he makes shoes as well as he plays cricket,' said the Prince, 'he shall be my shoemaker.'

☆

Another almost forgotten Royal cricketer was Prince Christian Victor, eldest son of Princess Helena, the second daughter of Queen Victoria. Between tours of military duty he played cricket and in India, in 1893, thought when he had scored 205 that he had made the highest score ever made in that country and threw away his wicket. Too late he discovered that he had needed another 13 runs to achieve that distinction.

Short Careers

H. T. Gamlin played only three games for Somerset, against Essex and Lancashire in July 1895 and one against Yorkshire in the following season. His career bowling average was 2 for 207 runs and his batting total amounted to 7, including four ducks followed by 2 and 5. Yet he has one claim to fame. He was the bowler when Archie MacLaren, of Lancashire, was caught by Fowler with his score at a record-breaking 424, the highest score ever achieved by an English batsman. At the time, Gamlin was just 17 years old.

...

J. C. W. MacBryan, of Somerset, had no chance of showing his undoubted skills – he was a county regular for several seasons – when he was selected to play for England v. South Africa at Manchester in 1924. The match was ruined by rain, he neither batted nor bowled and was never chosen for a Test side again.

☆

Five batsmen are listed in *The Kaye Book of Cricket Records* as scoring centuries in their only first-class match. The best was 207 by N. Callaway for New South Wales v. Queensland at Sydney in 1914–15.

...

One short and undistinguished career in the first-class game was mentioned in *Wisden* in 1965. Frederick J. Hyland, who died in February 1964, aged 70, had played one game as a professional for Northamptonshire v. Hampshire at Northampton in 1924. Play was limited by rain to two overs from which the home side scored one run without loss.

☆

Wisden's obituaries for 1978 devote only three lines to Sidney George Wills, whose first-class career was of comparable length. He was chosen as a batsman for Gloucestershire v. Kent at Bristol in 1927 but the match, his only appearance for the county, was abandoned without a ball being bowled.

Sixes

In 1952—53 M. Hockney hit eight sixes off an eight-ball over for Clare Blues v. Mintaro, in Adelaide, Australia. He missed a chance of further glory by failing to score off a no-ball. (*Cricket* by Rowland Bowen.) And, from the same source, it seems that Basil d'Oliveira, batting for Croxley v. Mariedahl in 1953—54, hit 28 sixes and ten fours in scoring 225 in 65 minutes. He hit his first five balls for sixes.

...

Wisden Cricket Monthly reported in September 1980 that 14 houses close to Darfield CC's ground, Yorkshire, had been fitted with bullet-proof glass to prevent further breakages from six hits.

☆

Following a court case in October 1965 Mr Justice Lyell decided that members of Egham CC, Surrey, should stop hitting sixes into the garden and swimming pool of a house adjoining the club's ground.

...

The *Daily Express* in its 'Just Fancy That' feature on 26 August 1970 told how a batsman playing for Moorside against Uppermill, in a league match near Oldham, Lancashire, hit a ball at a fielder, Alan Broadbent, who ducked. The ball bounced off his head and sailed into the pavilion for six and not the expected four. The extra two runs gave Moorside a win.

☆

When Sir Gary Sobers hit Malcolm Nash, of Glamorgan, for six sixes in one over at Swansea, the *Sunday Times* quoted the bowler as saying: 'I suppose I can gain some consolation from the fact that my name will be permanently in the record books.' Nash wanted to have the ball mounted but it was hit out of the ground and was not returned.

The previous best, five sixes in one over, had been done by A. W. Wellard off Woolley for Somerset v. Kent in 1938 and also against Derbyshire off T. R. Armstrong in 1936, and by J. D. Lindsay of the touring Fezela XI v. Essex in 1961 who punished W. T. Greensmith.

...

Wellard, the above-named Somerset smiter, made one quarter of his 12,000 runs in sixes. Even more impressive was another Somerset stalwart, H. Gimblett, who as an opening batsman hit 250 sixes.

☆

When the late Ken Barrington hit a six during a Sunday game at Reading CC's ground (said the *Daily Mail* on 8 August 1964) the ball landed on the pavilion roof and set fire to it. Presumably there was an electrical fault and the six sparked it off.

...

W. Hayman, playing for Bath Association against Thornbury in 1902, scored 359 not out in 100 minutes. He scored 32 in one over from E. M. Grace and altogether hit 32 sixes off him.

☆

Sixes have often hit and hurt people who weren't even watching cricket but on one occasion, so the story goes, a six from that great hitter, C. I. Thornton, smashed through the bedroom window of an elderly invalid who had been bedridden for 15 years. Apparently she fled downstairs, decided to live henceforth on the ground floor and led an active life for the next ten years.

The *Daily Telegraph* on 27 September 1966 recalled that the late
B. G. W. Atkinson, batting at Lord's for Middlesex, received a short
fast bouncer from Alf Gover which he hit back over the bowler's head
for six with an overhead smash, tennis style.

...

Cases of Australian champagne were offered by a local enthusiast at
Southend, Essex, in 1956 to anyone hitting a ball into a lake situated
about 100 yards from the pitch. At that time the last winner had been
Gerry German, the Essex amateur bowler, who celebrated his debut at
no.11 by hitting a delivery from Jim Laker for six into the water.

Stumps and Bails

Wisden's obituary of Arthur Woodcock, the Leicestershire fast bowler who died in 1910, relates how, when bowling for MCC against Lewes Priory in 1908 on the Dripping Pan, Lewes, Sussex, he hit the stumps with such force that he knocked a bail 149 feet 6 inches.

...

A Mr Rotherham, of Uppingham, a fast bowler for Rutlandshire, once struck a bail into the next county – but the county boundary line was only 62 yards away.

☆

Newspapers on 31 May 1950 told how, in cutting a ball from R. O. Jenkins, the Worcestershire spin-bowler, D. J. Insole, with his score at 105, brought his bat down on the off stumps with such force that he broke a bail. He was, of course, given out hit wicket.

...

When weather conditions are such that the bails refuse to stay on various methods are used to keep them in place. At Kurri, near Newcastle, Australia, stated the Express News Service on 15 November 1962, chewing gum was used. Weighted bails were used at Trent Bridge on 3 July 1961. 'Wind-cheater' bails solved the problem on the Chatham ground in a match between Combined Services and a touring Canadian XI. These were made of lignum vitae – the stuff bowls are made of – and weighed twice as much as orthodox bails.

☆

'Ward's Folly' or the 'Barndoor Match' is the name often given to the Gentlemen v. Players encounter in July 1837. In the hope of giving the Gentlemen a better chance of winning they defended stumps of the usual size, but the Players took guard before stumps 38 inches by 12 inches. That made no difference as the Players still won by an innings.

In 1956 Mr Herbert Haydon, of Weston-super-Mare, demonstrated at Lord's his stumps, which were quite different from the traditional kind. His were orange-coloured 'to show up better'. They screwed into the ground instead of having to be knocked in and the bails were quite unorthodox. They fitted not into grooves but onto buttons. The bails were ringed at one end, to fit over the two outer stumps, but were only half ringed to fit round the middle stump. Their inventor claimed that his stumps would be firmer rooted and that the bails would fall at the slightest touch, although immovable in windy conditions. MCC officials told Mr Haydon that his stumps conformed to the Laws of the game and that it was up to him to persuade county and club sides to adopt them.

...

The same newspaper report stated that Lord's is 'quite a repository of inventions'. One is a set of aluminium bails pierced with holes to allow wind to pass through and not blow them off. When they were tried the bails were quite satisfactory, except that wicket-keepers didn't like them much. They whistled distractingly.

☆

Several varieties of patent stumps have been invented, in most of which the stumps returned automatically to an upright position by the action of springs in their sockets. In one set invented in 1865 the stumps were connected to a wooden frame by ball-and-socket joints, the bails being fastened to them with small chains.

...

To show his contempt for some bowlers the Rev. Lord Frederick Beauclerck, DD, vicar of St Albans, used to hang an expensive gold watch from his middle stump. (Carr's *Dictionary of Extra-ordinary English Cricketers*.)

☆

Playing for MCC v. Yorkshire at Lord's in 1870 C. R. Filgate had the unusual experience of seeing all three stumps knocked out of the ground by a delivery from Freeman.

During a match in India, a writer in *Everybody's* for 9 September 1938 stated, termites burrowed into a set of stumps, leaving them completely hollow though outwardly unharmed. They were left in place on the pitch overnight and crumbled to dust the next day the first time they were touched.

...

Instances of a ball hitting the stumps but not dislodging the bails are not uncommon but A. E. Stoddart, playing for Middlesex v. Surrey at the Oval in 1895, had a unique experience. In the first innings he was given out stumped but, as the bails had not been dislodged, he was allowed to bat on and scored 75. In the second innings a ball from F. E. Smith hit his stumps quite hard, yet did not dislodge the bails and Stoddart went on to score 67.

☆

Cricket reporters noted Neil Harvey's remarkable escape on 26 October 1950 when playing in a district match in Melbourne. With his score at 17 Harvey appeared to be clean bowled when a fast bowler hit his middle stump. 'Both bails flew into the air, but fell back into the grooves on the stumps.' Harvey set off for the pavilion but the umpire recalled him, saying he was not out as the bails must fall to the ground.

...

In the local derby between Thornaby and Stockton in the North Yorkshire and South Durham League, the *Northern Echo* reported on 23 July 1956, J. Hunter bowled Ray Bell middle stump without removing either bail. The two bails, presumably rather gluey because of the heat, remained suspended between leg and off stumps with the middle stump flat on the ground.

☆

A Mr E. Winter about 150 years ago tried to cut a ball, missed, and drove the bails deep between the spreadeagled stumps. The umpires consulted for a while and then gave him not out.

An article by W. J. Ford in the *Strand Magazine* for June 1901 tells how, in a match played at Hastings, C. A. Alberga was batting when the wind blew his handkerchief from his belt and twisted it round the wicket without removing a bail.

…

In a match in 1911 R. D. Burrows was cut in the face when a ball from J. H. King (Leicestershire) hit the stumps and the bails flew forward.

☆

When two Australian clubs, Glebe and Cumberland, met in 1932 the latter team's fast bowler, Charlie Nicholls, sent down a ball that beat Coffey of Glebe. It just nicked the off bail, knocking it off and, quick as a flash, Coffey picked it up and replaced it, pretending that the wind had blown it off. No one objected and Coffey went on to make 48, top score for his side. (*Six and Out*, compiled by Jack Pollard.)

…

The same book tells how, when the Australians once toured Canada, they played at Moosejaw where the rules were slightly adjusted. 'Chewing gum parked on top of the stumps proved a great help to Moosejaw batsmen, who were regarded as not out if the bails merely hung down instead of falling.'

☆

At Old Trafford S. Madan Lal, playing for India in the first Test in 1974, was clean bowled by Hendrick for 2. The off and leg stumps were knocked out of the ground, but the middle one was left standing.

…

Batting for Middlesex against Sussex at Lord's in 1893 C. P. Foley picked up a fallen bail and was given out by the umpire. The Sussex captain then recalled him.

☆

In 1930 C. C. Case, batting for Somerset against Nottinghamshire at Taunton, was out 'hit wicket b. Voce'. He fell onto his stumps and was so confused that he left the field carrying under his arm not his bat but a stump.

Tombstones

The tombstone erected over the grave of John Willes, inventor of round-arm bowling, unlike those of several other noted cricketers, tells its story in words only. On it is carved the inscription: 'To the memory of John Willes Eqr., of Bellingham in this parish. Born 1777, died 1852, at Staunton, near Gloucester. He was a patron of all manly sports and the first to introduce round-arm bowling in cricket. This memorial is erected by the few friends who remember him as a genuine sportsman, staunch friend, kind neighbour and genial companion.'

...

More often a more graphic method is used to indicate the fame of a cricketer over whose grave the tombstone stands. When part of Highgate cemetery, London, was bought by a conservation society early in 1981 the *Daily Telegraph* mentioned that 'Lillywhite, the cricketer, has a headstone depicting shattered stumps and a broken column signifying the end of life's innings'. Presumably this was Frederic William Lillywhite, who died of cholera in London in 1854.

☆

In similar style is the tombstone in Eyam churchyard, Derbyshire, over the grave of Harry Bagshaw, famous in his day as a bowler and later an umpire. An umpire's hand with finger raised, signalling 'Out', decorates the top and underneath is a set of stumps, with bails flying, and bat and ball. When he was buried in 1927 Harry Bagshaw was wearing his umpire's coat and had a cricket ball in his hand.

...

R. G. Barlow, the stonewalling Lancashire batsman, was buried in Blackpool and he, it is said, chose his tombstone before he died. It shows one of the bails knocked from the stumps and above it are the words, 'Bowled at Last'. In a panel below is the one word, 'Barlow'. For several years before his death in 1919 Barlow lived in a house in Woodland Grove, Blackpool, and over the front door was a carved representation of stumps and a bat.

Barlow's companion of many innings, A. N. Hornby, was buried in Acton churchyard, near Nantwich, Cheshire, and his stone is engraved with stumps, bat and ball and, very unusually, a facsimile of his signature.

☆

Fuller Pilch, one of the greatest cricketers of the early nineteenth century, lies in the churchyard of St Gregory in Canterbury. His is a large tomb and an obelisk 12 feet high shows a batsman with his middle stump knocked out. The inscription lauds Pilch for 'his skill as a cricketer, and his worth as a Man'.

...

In some instances graves not marked by tombstones mark the last resting-place of cricketers whose love for the game was demonstrated at their funerals. Daniel Day, whose cricketing took him from Hampshire to Northumberland and back to Southampton, and who died in 1887 at the age of 80, directed that his bat, pads and walking stick should be placed in his coffin with him. John Bowyer, of Surrey, had his bat nailed to his coffin.

☆

In *A New Book of Epitaphs* R. L. Brown includes one entitled 'The Salisbury Cricketer' which reads as follows:

> 'I bowl'd, I struck, I caught, I stopp'd.
> Sure life's a game of cricket;
> I block'd with care, with caution popp'd,
> Yet Death has hit my wicket.'

Umpires

Years ago, in Hyde Park, Sydney, an umpire named Bogg was killed by a batsman who took a wild swipe at the ball, missed and hit him. And in 1878 at Pyrmont another umpire was killed in the same way. Presumably in both cases the umpire was standing close to the wicket and the delivery was a wide one.

...

In July 1966 the *Daily Sketch* mentioned that George Palfreman, an umpire in a local Bradford league, had reported himself to the appropriate authorities for allowing an 18-ball over when Bankfoot and Baildon second XI met at Odsal. He no-balled six of Geoffrey Robb's first seven deliveries, passed the next five as all right and allowed him to continue bowling until Robb had sent down 18 balls.

☆

William Gunn (Nottinghamshire), a member of the team that visited Australia in 1886–87, while playing in the Test at Sydney acted as umpire for part of the match (*The Times*, 25 February 1971). The same report mentions Jem Phillips, an Australian umpire, who 'made a habit of commuting between Australia and England and umpired in both lands'.

...

A number of amusing stories are told of Bill Reeves when umpiring. A man given out by him lbw complained, 'Bill, that was never out in this world. It pitched miles outside.' To which Reeves replied, 'Look in tonight's paper and see whether it's out or not.' On another occasion a batsman who had hooked a ball to the boundary realised that he had displaced a bail with the seat of his trousers. Replacing it, he found Reeves at his shoulder. 'A bit windy today, Mr Reeves,' he remarked. 'It is that,' agreed Reeves. 'Mind it doesn't blow your cap off on your way to the pavilion.'

Playing at Bolney, Sussex, in June 1972 one of the home team crashed a ball against the square-leg umpire's shin from where it rebounded to a fielder who ran out the batsman. When one of the visitors enquired after the umpire's leg he was told, 'I'm all right, I've a wooden leg.'

☆

Alec Skelding was another umpire with a nice turn of wit. Apparently Jim Sims, of Middlesex, having had difficulty in dealing with off-spinners, decided in one game to play them from a foot wide of the leg stump. Arriving at the wicket, he placed his bat well away from the stumps in the direction of square leg and said, 'Where am I, Alec?' To which Skelding replied, 'You're at Marble Arch. You need a taxi.'

...

One umpire in a game on the Isle of Wight was reported for giving a wrong lbw decision. Complainants said that he was a notorious thief who had spent a lifetime of dishonesty and whose word could not be trusted. The occasion was a match between the Habitual Criminals XI and the South of England Pickpockets at Parkhurst Prison, Isle of Wight, and was described in *College Harry* by David Elias, the auto-biography of an old lag.

☆

According to an old magazine, the earliest code of cricket rules remained in force until 1774 as 'Ye Game of Cricket as settled by ye Cricket Club at ye Star and Garter in Pall Mall'. The umpires were described as the 'sole judges of all outs and ins, of all fair and unfair play, of frivolous delays, of all hurts, whether real or pretended, and are discretionally to allow whatever time they think proper before ye Game goes on again. In case of a real hurt to a striker they are to allow another to come in, and to allow the Person hurt to come in again, but are not to allow a fresh Man to play on either side on any Account. They are the sole judges of all hindrances, crossing ye Players in running and standing unfair to Striker and in case of hindrance may order a notch to be scored ... Each umpire is ye Sole Judge of all Nips and Catches, ins and outs, good or bad runs ... and he shall not be changed for another umpire without ye consent of both sides.'

113

Advice given by George Parr, the old Nottinghamshire stalwart, to young cricketers: 'When you play in a match, be sure not to forget to pay a little attention to the umpire. First of all, inquire after his health, then say what a fine player his father was, and finally present him with a brace of birds or rabbits. This will give you confidence and you will probably do well.'

...

Another Bill Reeves story. In a county match some years ago a young amateur playing for an unspecified county was facing A. P. Freeman, the Kent slow bowler, and was in all sorts of trouble. In desperation he lunged forward at every ball but made no contact. Eventually he was hit on the pad and on appeal was given out. During the interval the dismissed batsman sat next to Reeves and said: 'Mr Reeves, I didn't think I was out lbw. I was playing so far forward.' To which Bill replied, 'No, I don't think you were out either, but you were making such a fool of yourself I thought you'd be better back in the pavilion.'

☆

Umpires have occasionally, when a wicket fell at the end of an over, allowed the bowler to send down several more deliveries in error. But there seems to be only one instance of a bowler getting short measure. During Freddie Trueman's innings for Yorkshire v. Hampshire at Leeds in May 1961, the umpire, Fred Jakeman, was so bewitched by the batsman's onslaught on Peter Sainsbury – 2, 6, 6, 2, 4 – that he apparently lost count.

...

The first match between Lancashire and Gloucestershire, played at Old Trafford in July 1878, was marked by an incident in which the crowd persuaded an umpire to reverse his decision. A contemporary account reported: 'Mr Patterson [of Lancashire] drove a ball to the boundary; the umpire not seeing if it went there, did not call ''four'', but some spectators did, so the batters stopped running, and before he got home Mr Patterson's wicket was put down, the umpire giving him [run] out. An objection was raised, the game stopped, and two captains held a long consultation, but the matter was not settled until Dr Grace went to where the ball was hit to, and questioned those who saw it, when they all satisfactorily stated that the ball had passed beyond the bounds, so Mr Patterson resumed his innings.'

The Weather

The first match of the 1981 season between Cambridge University and Essex hit the headlines because of the weather. It didn't snow but the umpires after consultation with the captains invoked Law 3, subsection 14(d), which states: 'The umpires should suspend play only when they consider conditions are so bad that it is unreasonable or dangerous to continue.' On this occasion, 24 April, the day was so cold that one batsman could not see because the bitter wind and contact lenses were making his eyes water. Bowlers could not grasp the ball properly and Ken McEwan wore a batting helmet with the visor down to act as a windshield. After lunch, the old, familiar announcement was made: match abandoned – rain.

...

Snow in much milder conditions has interfered with play on several occasions. On 1 May 1967 snow held up play at Nottingham, Derby, Edgbaston and Cambridge, hail sent players running for shelter at Oxford and there was thunder at other places.

☆

At Kendal, Cumbria, snow stopped play in May 1955, the pitch being covered with it in ten minutes. On 24 May 1962 'a spectacular hailstorm' blew down both sight-screens, flooded the pitch and ended operations for the day when Hampshire had made 226 for 4 in answer to Leicestershire's 315 for 8 declared. And under 20 April the 1958 MCC Diary stated: 'Fiftieth anniversary of W. G. Grace's last first-class match; Gentlemen of England v. Surrey, the Oval; play stopped by snow.'

...

The scorebooks for the East Bierley v. Farsley match in the Bradford League in June 1954 noted that 'wind stopped play'. The umpires called a halt when the wind had become too strong for play to be possible. Presumably the wind died down considerably for the report in *The Cricketer* states that Farsley eventually won the match.

An East Yorkshire Cup match at Scarborough between Driffield and Scarborough 'A' on 28 May 1951 was abandoned because of fog. One player commented, 'We've never known a game to end like this. You could see the ball until it pitched, then it was lost in a blanket of fog.' The fog was so thick that people in the pavilion were kept informed of the game's progress by an outfielder near the scorebox. Scarborough 'A', batting first, made 239 for 3 and Driffield's score at close of play was 86 for 5.

☆

A paragraph in the *Evening Despatch* for 9 September 1959 recalled the rainy summer of 1931 when '17 inches of rain fell in five months – compared with an average of only 28 inches for the whole year'. It continued: 'On August 6 of that year, for example, the cricket match between Warwickshire and New Zealand at Edgbaston was held up for 40 minutes – by fog.'

...

On 27 January 1963 two teams played on the frozen lake in the grounds of Lullingstone Castle, Kent. They 'found it a very sticky wicket indeed, in the thaw yesterday,' ran one report. 'Indeed, towards the end of the game square leg sank.'

☆

Usually protests of too much sun come from batsmen who are dazzled not by the sun itself but by its rays being reflected from car windscreens (Essex v. Derbyshire at Romford, 30 May 1963; Leicestershire v. Oxford University at Leicester, 24 June 1969). The umpires had to ask people at a nearby factory to pull down the blinds on some windows when Derbyshire played Worcestershire at Derby on 8 June 1967, and play ended 15 minutes early.

...

At Derby on 28 April 1967 the visitors, Leicestershire, appealed against bad light and play was suspended for ten minutes. When they returned they complained again that the sunlight was blinding them and the game ended five minutes early.

116

In the second Test at Lord's between India and England in June 1959 Manjrekar asked for a camera in the pavilion to be covered because the sun on the lens was dazzling him. And *The Times* reported on 15 May 1967 that a batsman at Lord's 'unsighted by a reflection from an unknown source' protested and the culprit was eventually tracked down. It was a large clergyman whose pectoral cross was dazzling him.

☆

And in less exalted circles the Offwell CC in Devon had to cancel a match in August 1955. Sunshine had cracked the pitch and made it too dangerous for play.

…

Cricket is regularly played at Christmas by enthusiasts at Brighton and in Yorkshire, but always on terra firma. The winter of 1878–79, described in *Wisden* as 'long, sad and severe', began in October 1878 and lasted until the middle of May 1879. This enabled 'more cricket matches on the ice to be played than ever before in the course of one winter'. In his *Wisden Anthology 1864–1900* Benny Green gives details or scores of eight matches and this 'does not comprise all the matches so played'. One at Windsor was played by moonlight on a frozen lake in the Home Park. Mr Bowditch's side, of which only nine men batted, scored 15 to Mr Gage's side in which ten men batted and knocked up 17.

☆

On an earlier occasion, an old writer reported, W. G. Grace played in a game on the frozen surface of the lake in Windsor Great Park, scored a brilliant century and took five wickets.

…

Lack of sun is a constant complaint at cricket matches but on several occasions play has been suspended because of too much sun, while the Surrey v. Lancashire match at the Oval in 1868 was stopped for an hour because of the great heat.

☆

A correspondent reminded readers of *Wisden Cricket Monthly* in the July 1981 issue that the game in which Cambridge University and Essex players left the field because of the intense cold on 24 April 1981 was not unique. Apparently during the Gentlemen v. Players match at Hastings in 1903 'the players, overcome by the cold, left the field for a little while'.

Women and Cricket

Two women, one of whom apparently never played cricket, had a lasting influence on the game. Christina Willes, who lived near Canterbury in the early nineteenth century, often bowled to her brother John in a barn during the winter. Because of her voluminous skirts she could not bowl orthodox underarm, but had to use a sort of half round-arm style. This demanded a different batting technique which John Willes practised. He also thought Christina's bowling would make scoring more difficult and in 1807 he introduced it into some games in which he took part. It met with great opposition. Batsmen objected, umpires no-balled him and spectators often invaded the field and pulled up the stumps. For fifteen years Willes persevered, gaining some support, but when he tried the new-style bowling at Lord's in July 1822 between Kent and MCC he was again no-balled. This time he left the field, mounted his horse and rode away, out of cricket for ever. However, he did train other players, notably near Sutton Valence, in Kent, among them the famous Alfred Mynn. Round-arm bowling was eventually recognised as fair, later developing into overarm – and all because of a young lady's skirts.

...

The other lady was none other than Mrs H. M. Grace (the only woman listed in *Wisden*'s 'Births and Deaths of Cricketers'), mother of W. G. Grace. She wrote to George Parr suggesting that he found a place for her son, E. M. Grace, in his All England XI. She also said that, although E. M. was already renowned for his hard hitting and big scores, she had another son who would be even better – William Gilbert Grace.

☆

Women's cricket is no longer something to be laughed at. After being ignored as a suitable pastime for ladies for many years it began to revive in 1926 with the formation of the Women's Cricket Association and by July 1929 a match was played between London and District and the Rest of England. A few years later women cricketers embarked on a series of overseas tours which now form a recognised feature of the game.

The first women's cricket match of which there are records was played on Gosden Common, near Guildford, Surrey, on 26 July 1745 between 'eleven maids of Bramley and eleven maids of Hambleton, dressed all in white. The Bramley maids had blue ribbon and the Hambleton maids red ribbons on their heads. The Bramley team lost, scoring only 119 notches to their opponents' 127.'

...

In 1772 someone arranged 'a whimsical match, viz. that 11 women from Hants. shall play, some time this month, with twice the number of Hampton gentlemen, for £500, and what is not a little singular, the odds, it is asserted, are already considerable in favour of the female professors of that noble exercise'. Unfortunately the result of the contest, if indeed if took place, has never been discovered.

☆

The year 1811 saw a match between 11 women of Surrey, captained by Ann Baker, aged 60 and said to be the best runner and bowler of her team, and 11 from Hampshire. 'The combatants were clad in loose trowsers, with short-fringed petticoats descending to the knees, and light flannel waistcoats with sashes round the waist,' says a contemporary report. Despite her repute Ann's team lost by 14 runs on Monday 7 October after play had been suspended because of rain.

...

Many more all-women matches took place and in 1887 the White Heather Club was founded by eight titled ladies. Four years later it had 50 members, among them Miss Lucy Ridsdale, who later became Countess Baldwin. According to Maurice Golesworthy's *Encyclopaedia of Cricket* it was disbanded in 1958 by which time women's cricket as we know it was firmly established.

☆

The Gillette Book of Cricket and Football states that, not far from Christchurch, New Zealand, there was a picturesque little cricket ground called, equally picturesquely, 'The Valley of Peace'. Because of the beauty of its surroundings? Not a bit of it – because no woman had ever been permitted to set foot on its masculine turf.

The women of Bentley, near Ipswich, took over the local men's team that had disbanded some years before. 'Their opening bats,' said one report, 'are Mrs Gaye Strutt and her mother-in-law, Lady Belper. At the weekend they played another women's club in the first-ever match and won by 20 runs. Mrs Strutt knocked up 48. She remarked: ''The men laughed at us – but they were not sufficiently go-ahead to get up a team themselves.'' ' A footnote to this statement mentioned that 'Bentley CC bowls underarm – but hopes to have perfected overarm bowling in time for next season.'

...

A sad note headlined '£20 All Out' was sounded by the *Daily Express* on 27 September 1972. It stated that the women's cricket club at Dunton Bassett, Leicestershire, which had gone 25 years without a fixture, had been wound up. Founded in 1937, it regularly played other women's teams for ten years and then members lost interest. The remaining funds, £20, were handed over to an old people's organisation.

☆

Detective-Constable Marilyn Evans was pictured in the *Daily Mail* of 30 May 1981 under the caption 'Easy Catch for Girl Detective'. Not only was she the star wicket-keeper of her ladies' team in Devon, she was registered with a policemen's team as a likely player. She also umpires men's matches.

Miscellaneous

During the Australians' visit to the West Indies in 1964–65 a correspondent in *The Guardian* told how, during a match at Sabina Park, a man stood all morning outside the ground with a rope fastened to the top of the wall and charged anyone who could not get into the ground in the usual way five cents to climb up and jump over. Business was so good that during the lunch interval he had to go home and empty his pockets of five-cent pieces.

...

Arthur Haygarth, compiler of *Cricket Scores and Biographies of Celebrated Cricketers*, obtained much of his information by taking notes from the tombstones of players long dead and from parish registers in southern counties. When old age began to tell he asked Robert Thoms, an umpire, to visit other churchyards to record more inscriptions. He offered £1.50 a week, plus expenses – good remuneration in those days – but Thoms refused, saying: 'Tombstones never appealed strongly to me.'

☆

Wisden records only eleven instances of batsmen being dismissed 'hit the ball twice'. It overlooks one mentioned in Rowland Bowen's *Cricket* where he states that 'Jasper Vinall was killed accidentally at Horsted Keynes, through attempting to hit the ball twice to avoid being caught'.

...

Mowing machines were first used at Lord's between 1850 and 1855, but the advantages of having the grass cut mechanically instead of relying on sheep grazing there did not appeal to the Hon. Robert Grimston. When he arrived at the ground and saw the new-fangled machines in use he offered some navvies a handful of sovereigns to interrupt the work and smash the mowers with their pickaxes.

Several sources confirm that when cricket was introduced into Samoa it was so popular that in 1890 it was banned by law, because people neglected their crops in order to play. The ban was lifted but re-imposed when the islanders, after natural disasters, were more interested in cricket than in re-building their shattered homes.

☆

J. W. H. T. Douglas, the old Essex and England captain, fielded without a hat or cap in all weathers. It was widely believed that he was immune from sunstroke.

…

'John Kinloch (of Sydney) was a star underarm bowler. As he was near-sighted, Kinloch always wore a monocle when playing.' (Johnnie Moyes in *Six and Out*.)

'Three Men Out with One Ball' was a headline in one national newspaper on 25 May 1958. Ted Lester, playing for Yorkshire Colts v. Northants second XI at Barnsley, was caught out at deep extra cover by Jim Edmonds just as Mick Norman dashed up to try for it. They collided and Edmonds, who held the catch, was knocked unconscious. Norman was concussed, and his leg spiked by Edmonds' cricket boot. He was taken to hospital, Edmonds recovered and Lester was out.

☆

Sir Frank Benson, a great cricket fan, once inserted an advertisement in a stage paper stating: 'Wanted: actor to play Laertes and Lysander, preferably a slow left-arm bowler. Apply the Benson Company.'

...

The Derbyshire v. Yorkshire match at Chesterfield in 1946 began on an oversized pitch. After two overs Len Hutton queried its length so it was re-measured and found to be two yards too long. The match was restarted when the stumps had been resited the proper distance apart. The incident is not unique. During the Cambridge University v. C. I. Thornton's XI match at Cambridge on 18 May 1885 two men on the visitors' team had been dismissed when it was discovered that the stumps were a yard and a quarter too far apart and this match was restarted.

☆

George Duckworth, the Lancashire and England wicket-keeper, was fond of telling how in the Test at Leeds in 1930, when Sir Donald Bradman scored 334, he himself scored 33 in an innings that was spread over three days because of interruptions by rain.

...

Only one batsman has scored precisely 1,000 runs in May. He was Charles Hallows, the Lancashire opener, who scored exactly that number.

The Rev. F. N. Bird, according to *Wisden*, played cricket for five counties – Gloucestershire, Northamptonshire, Buckinghamshire, Devon and Suffolk. W. Montgomery played for Surrey, Somerset, Wiltshire, Cheshire and Hertfordshire.

☆

Only one man has been decorated for bravery on a cricket field. He was Colonel Douglas Brett, whose death was reported in the *Daily Telegraph* on 2 January 1964. In 1934, while he was playing in a match at Chittagong, five Hindu terrorists carrying bombs and a pistol suddenly attacked players and spectators. He tackled the gunmen and for his bravery was awarded the Empire Gallantry Medal. Holders of this decoration were automatically awarded the George Medal when it was instituted in 1940.

...

Someone decided that Ken Barrington (Surrey) and Fred Titmus (Middlesex) were streets ahead of the other MCC tourists in Australia in 1965–66. A builder in Adelaide decided to name new streets after them – Barrington Crescent and Titmus Avenue.

☆

Although Yorkshire recruits only Yorkshire-born cricketers, two or three players born outside the county have in fact played for it. Most famous is Lord Hawke, who was born in Lincolnshire, W. G. Keighley, son of Bradford-born parents, was born in France, while one famous player appeared once or twice for Yorkshire before it was realised that he was not a 'native'. He was Cecil Parkin, who was born just over the border in Eaglescliffe, Co. Durham.

...

In its 'Births and Deaths of Cricketers', *Wisden* lists J. J. Bridges as being a Somerset player. True, but he had an unusual distinction that probably makes him unique in first-class cricket. In the 1919 season he started as an amateur, became a professional later on, but before the season ended was playing again as an amateur – a strange hat-trick.

David Harris, the old Hambledon stalwart, stricken by gout in his later years, had an armchair brought to the wicket when he was batting. After dealing with a delivery David sat down for a rest until the bowler was ready once more.

☆

Fred Root, who bowled for both Derbyshire and Worcestershire, played for England against Australia in three Tests in 1926 and never had a chance to bat.

...

The *Wisden* biography of George Edward Hemingway who died in 1907 tells how he once played in a single-wicket game against two brothers and he made a hit of about 250 runs. The ball ran into a bed of nettles and while his opponents argued about who should plunge and recover it he kept on running.

☆

In the 1870s the village of Chipstead, Wiltshire, cricket club used the hymn-board, lent by the local vicar, as its scoreboard. They also used the church vestry as a pavilion.

...

The temporary absence of most of the Nottinghamshire bowlers in a car crash prior to a game against Yorkshire at Leeds some years ago compelled the captain, A. W. Carr, to win the toss and knock up a big score. He told George Gunn to stay in until teatime. According to Neville Cardus, George said 'I'm sorry, Mr Carr, but I can't hold out that long. My legs are not what they used to be.' Carr would have none of that so George, promising to stay until 3.30 pm at least, eventually said he would hold out longer if he were paid an extra pound an hour. He stayed at the wicket until 5.30 pm for 40 runs and then surprised his skipper by asking for time and a half for the extra length of his innings. In all he got five pounds ten shillings.

Australian professional Ken Rogers, playing for Stalybridge, Cheshire, in 1955 refused to accept his match pay of £10 a match because he was off form. In his first game he took 3 for 38 and scored 7. In the next he did not bowl and failed to score, so again he refused his pay.

☆

The *Australian Cricketer* once claimed that Captain W. Ward, deputy master of the Australian Mint, when batting 'turned his posterior to the bowler and peered at him over his left shoulder, perplexing and confusing the bowler, who could never be sure that Ward was ready'.

...

The most famous cricket ignoramous was probably George Bernard Shaw who, being told that England had won the Australian Tests, asked 'What have they been testing?'

☆

In a Surrey v. Northants game just before the second world war the stumps at one end were not disturbed for an hour or more. The batsmen out had all been either caught or lbw. Eventually Ted Brooke, the Surrey wicket-keeper, examined them when a wicket did fall. He discovered that a spider had spun a web between the middle and off stumps.

Also in Unwin Paperbacks

PHOENIX FROM THE ASHES
The Story of the England-Australia Series 1981
Mike Brearley

Every so often the world of sport throws up an event or performance quite out of the ordinary. Cricket has had more than its fair share. What was so unusual about the events of 1981, however, was that it provided not one match but three which caught the public's imagination – and brought Test cricket back to a popularity it had not enjoyed since the Centenary Test of 1977.

In the Third Test at Headingley, England, seemingly about to lose the Ashes, came back from the brink of defeat to win by 18 runs. At Edgbaston, barely a fortnight later, England repeated the performance, bowling out Australia for 121 in their fourth innings, to win this time by 29. In the Fifth Test the margin was greater – 103 runs – but not before Australia had threatened to win the game with something to spare. The Sixth Test was a draw, but one which contained three centuries, Lillee's best Test performance ever (7 for 89) and a nail-biting finish. But beyond the actual results there was the spectacle of the series being turned on its head by the performance of one man – Ian Botham, who had failed in the first two Tests and yet who in the Third scored a magnificent 149 not out, in the Fourth took a match-winning 5 wickets for 11 runs, and in the Fifth scored one of the great centuries of all time, 118 in 123 minutes.

There have been remarkable series and remarkable matches before, but never has an England captain so much at the heart of his team's success, or so able to express the full story of that success, written his account with such honesty and perception.

TEST MATCH SPECIAL
Edited by Peter Baxter

The first radio cricket commentary was broadcast in 1922. *Test Match Special*, which broadcast ball-by-ball coverage for the first time in 1957, has over the years become an integral part of the English summer.

Its commentators have been described as a bunch of friends going to a cricket match and talking about it. They have endeared themselves to over a million listeners worldwide with their style that mixes lyrical description with dry wit, shrewd appraisal and bonhomie.

This book takes as its focus the 1980 season and builds upon it reminiscences of past disasters, drinks in the box, listeners' letters and, of course, 'Rain Stops Play'.

'a valuable and most readable book . . . naturally relies upon a lively narrative from the current commentary team; and those closely associated with them. You must certainly not pad up and allow this one to pass through to the wicket keeper.'

Sunday Telegraph

RAIN STOPS PLAY
Brian Johnston

Rain Stops Play brings together a hilarious collection of anecdotes, jokes and stories which have rocked the commentary box and tickled the cricketing audience. Brian Johnston is the 'acknowledged master of the gaff' and his stories are illustrated by cricket fanatic, Bill Tidy.

'full of fun . . . lavishly illustrated' *Liverpool Post*

'winning collection' *Sheffield Star*

Phoenix from the Ashes *Mike Brearley* £1.95 ☐
Test Match Special *Edited by Peter Baxter* £1.75 ☐
Rain Stops Play *Brian Johnston* £1.25 ☐

All these books are available at your local bookshop or newsagent, or can be ordered direct by post. Just tick the titles you want and fill in the form below.

_____

Name ....

Address ....

....

....

Write to Unwin Cash Sales, PO Box 11, Falmouth, Cornwall TR10 9EN.

Please enclose remittance to the value of the cover price plus:

UK: 45p for the first book plus 20p for the second book, thereafter 14p for each additional book ordered, to a maximum charge of £1.63.

BFPO and EIRE: 45p for the first book plus 20p for the second book and 14p for the next 7 books and thereafter 8p per book.

OVERSEAS: 75p for the first book plus 21p per copy for each additional book.

Unwin Paperbacks reserve the right to show new retail prices on covers, which may differ from those previously advertised in the text or elsewhere. Postage rates are also subject to revision.